"T.J. Cloutier is probably the premier tournament player in the world today."

Doyle "Texas Dolly" Brunson, two-time World Champion of Poker; author of *Super System* and *Super System 2*

"Tom McEvoy and T.J. Cloutier are an awesome team of hold'em players and writers."

*Phil Hellmuth, 1989 World Champion of Poker,*
*11 Gold Bracelets*

"Tom McEvoy's tournament advice is the best ever written."

*Barbara Enright, 1996 World Champion Pot -Limit Hold'em*

"If there is one player that all of us fear the most at the final table, it is T.J. Cloutier."

*Berry Johnston, 1986 World Champion of Poker*

"Nobody knows how to win poker tournaments better than McEvoy."

Russ Hamilton, 1994 World Champion of Poker

"T.J. is the best no-limit player on the tournament circuit today."

*Hans "Tuna" Lund, 1996 World Champion Ace-to-5 Lowball*

"T.J. Cloutier is heads and shoulders above anyone else...He is a legend...the greatest no-limit hold'em player in the world.

*Mansour Matloubi, 1990 World Champion of Po*

# CHAMPIONSHIP

# 107 HOLD'EM TOURNAMENT HANDS

# CHAMPIONSHIP
# 107
# HOLD'EM
## TOURNAMENT HANDS

### T.J. CLOUTIER & TOM McEVOY

# CARDOZA PUBLISHING

Cardoza Publishing is the foremost gaming and gambling publisher in the world with a library of more than 200 up-to-date and easy-to-read books and strategies. These authoritative works are written by the top experts in their fields and with more than 10,000,000 books in print, represent the best-selling and most popular gaming books anywhere.

**NEW EDITION!**
Copyright © 2003, 2005, 2011 by Tom McEvoy, T. J. Cloutier, Dana Smith

Library of Congress Catalog Number: 2010933128
ISBN 10:     1-58042-268-3
ISBN 13: 978-1-58042-268-0

Visit our website or write for a full list of Cardoza Publishing books and advanced strategies.

## CARDOZA PUBLISHING
P.O. Box 98115, Las Vegas, NV 89193
Toll-Free Phone (800)577-WINS
email: cardozabooks@aol.com
**www.cardozabooks.com**

## ABOUT THE AUTHORS

**T.J. Cloutier** was inducted into the Poker Hall of Fame in 2006. He won the Player of the Year award in 1998 and 2002, and is considered to be one of the best tournament players in the world. Cloutier has won six World Series of Poker bracelets, and has appeared at the final table of the WSOP Main Event a remarkable four times, placing second in 1985 and in 2000. Overall, he has won more titles in no-limit and pot-limit hold'em than any other tournament player in the history of poker. Cloutier is the author of *How to Win the Championship*, and the co-author (with Tom McEvoy) of *Championship No-Limit & Pot-Limit Hold'em*, *Championship Omaha*, *Championship Hold'em* and *Championship Tournament Practice Hands*.

**Tom McEvoy**, the "Champion of Champions" has one of the most storied tournament careers of any poker player in history. In addition to winning four WSOP gold bracelets including the Main Event championship in 1983, McEvoy won the inaugural Champion of Champions tournament at the 2009 World Series of Poker in competition against the other living winners of the World Championship of Poker. He also won the 2005 Professional Poker Tour tournament sponsored by the World Poker Tour—an exclusive invitation-only event featuring the best players in the world—becoming the first player ever to win a PPT championship *and* a WSOP main event championship. A pioneer in improving conditions for poker players by sponsoring the nonsmoking movement in poker venues, McEvoy is the author and co-author of more than twelve other titles.

# TABLE OF CONTENTS

# PART TWO
## KEY HANDS AT THE WORLD SERIES OF POKER

# PART THREE
## LIMIT HOLD'EM HANDS
## INTRODUCTION

# FOREWORD

## Dana Smith

This book will help you win no-limit and limit hold'em tournaments by taking you inside the heads of Tom McEvoy and T.J. Cloutier as they think their way through the correct strategy for playing hold'em hands. Understanding the processes that champions use to win tournaments will give you the edge on your competition.

*Championship 107 Tournament Hands* provides two types of instruction designed to help you become a better tournament player. First, the action hands explain how champions use their skill and intuition to play strategically for maximum profit. Second, the key hands from the World Series of Poker demonstrate how world-class players have played in do-or-die situations. The authors' goal in giving you their analyses of these key hands is to help you gain useful insights into how tournament poker is played at the highest level.

Tournaments are harder than ever to win, partly because the playing fields these days are often huge. For example, 108 players entered the $10,000 championship event at the World Series of Poker in 1983, the year that Tom McEvoy won the title. In 1985, when T.J. Cloutier placed second in the title event, there were 140 entries. In 2000 when T.J. again finished second, the field had mushroomed to 512 entries, and by 2009 when 21-year-old Joe Cada won the championship, the number of entrants had ballooned to 6,494!

Big buy-in tournaments have proliferated as well. Casinos across the nation are hosting major events with buy-ins from

$1,000 to $10,000. With the advent of the World Poker Tour in 2002, $10,000 tournaments expanded to member casinos such as the Commerce Casino in Los Angeles, with the $25,000 buy-in championship event played at Bellagio in Las Vegas. No longer was the World Series of Poker the biggest game in town.

Another reason why it's hard to win tournaments these days is because the level of expertise of tournament players has increased dramatically. When I asked Doyle Brunson whether the World Series of Poker was tougher to beat today, he said, "Oh, sure. The players are so good. I mean, those kids have learned all the tournament moves, they know how to play."

How did they learn to play so well so fast? Many of today's whizzes have honed their skills online, where they are able to play more hands in one year than the older pros played in ten years. Further, most of the young tournament players I've interviewed over the years started playing low-limit tournaments for practice, read every book on tournament strategy, observed how the masters of poker played the game, continually analyzed their own play, and then added their special touch as they graduated to higher levels.

The tournament playing field is no longer even—that's the bottom line. Serious tournament poker players are putting more time, talent, and money at risk than ever before. Today you must outplay smarter and more experienced players, including many professionals, in bigger fields with higher buy-ins.

Tom and T.J. want to help you move up the ladder. We sincerely believe that studying the way they think about how to play major hands in challenging situations will enable you to join them in the winners' circle far sooner than you ever imagined.

PART ONE

# NO-LIMIT HOLD'EM TOURNAMENT HANDS

No-limit hold'em is today's biggest tournament game. We have television, the Internet, satellites, pocket cams, and Chris Moneymaker to thank for the explosion in popularity of poker's most thrilling game. In what other game can an amateur parlay a $39 satellite win into a $2.5 million payday, as Moneymaker did in his 2003 championship run?

"If he can do it, I can do it!" is the idea that has encouraged millions of novice poker players to take a shot at international fame and instant wealth by playing no-limit hold'em tournaments.

And why not? All it takes is skill, practice, good judgment, a lot of heart, and a little bit of luck.

Because so many people are entering no-limit hold'em tournaments in this new age of poker, you'll be facing players who have a wider range of tournament skill levels than ever before—from rank beginners to aggressive online players to seasoned pros. You can't depend on your opponents to play by the book and make standard moves at the pot these days, so making the right decision in every hand you play is more important than ever, especially when you're putting your entire stack of chips at risk every time you enter a pot.

You don't have to win a lot of pots in no-limit hold'em— you just need to win most of the pots you play. And to win those pots, you cannot afford to make mistakes. When you can lose all your chips in the play of just one hand, only one or two errors in judgment are enough to doom your chances of winning or even finishing in the money.

We have designed the tournament hands in this section to help you understand and practice the decision-making skills you need to win no-limit hold'em tournaments. By studying these hands, you will better understand the mental processes that professional no-limit hold'em players use to determine the best way to play certain types of hands in various situations against different types of opponents.

Look at each hand and think about how you would play it given the different situations we set up for you. Then read the analysis that T.J. gives for the play of the hand and compare it with your ideas. Let's kick things off with how to play pocket aces in different tournament situations.

# WINNING WITH POCKET ACES

How you play big pocket pairs depends on your position at the table, the rank of your pocket pair, the action in front and behind you, the board cards, and the nature of your opponents. In this chapter, we will take a look at various ways you might play aces, followed by how to play kings, queens and jacks in our next chapter. In each example, Player A is the first to act, Player B is the next, and Player C is last.

## WHEN YOU HAVE A-A IN EARLY POSITION

There's an old saying in poker that aces win small pots and lose big pots. In this section you'll see that this old adage is a fallacy—*when* you play aces the right way in *all* situations. Let's start with how to play A-A from a front position.

There are two schools of thought on how to play aces from a front position. A lot of players like to limp with two aces in the hope that someone will raise and give them the chance to play back at them so they can win a raised pot. They might win it right there, or they might get played with and wind up winning a huge pot. I don't like to give any free cards, so I prefer playing aces the second way—raising with them right away.

## The Case for Limping

If you limp with two aces and nobody raises behind you, you should not lose any more money than you've already put into the pot if the flop is bad for your hand. If someone swings at the pot after the flop, you can release the hand. What have you lost? Nothing except the original bet that you limped in with.

However, I've seen a lot of players limp in with aces, get a flop such as 7-6-5—and then an opponent who got in cheap with something like 6-5 or 9-8 swings at the pot, and the player who limped with A-A pays him off. That is not a good idea.

Either don't let him in preflop or, if you do limp in, play it strong if you think you have the best hand. Otherwise, let it go.

## ACTION HAND 1

### Limping with A-A in Early Position

Suppose you limp in with pocket aces preflop and get three or four callers. The flop comes:

### YOUR HAND

### FLOP

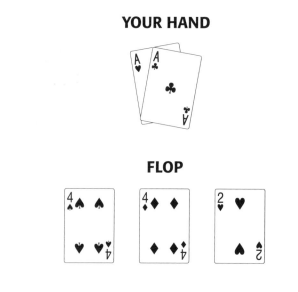

Any time a pair comes on the board when you've limped preflop, be leery. Or, suppose the flop contains three middle connectors such as:

## YOUR HAND

## FLOP

Or, what if it comes with three suited cards that don't match either of your aces:

## YOUR HAND

## FLOP

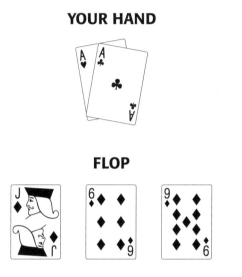

These types of flops can easily trip you up when you limp with aces preflop, so be very careful how you play on the flop.

When you limp in before the flop and no one raises, there will always be random blind hands that can show you any two cards, so that you never know whether an opponent has hit something on the flop. But if you bring it in for a raise, you can more accurately put your opponents on certain hands, and you at least have a better chance of taking them off their hands.

## The Case for Raising

You want to limit the field when you play big pairs so that, ideally, you can play against only one or two opponents. When you raise before the flop, you usually will have only one opponent. You know that you have the best hand to start with, and even though you might get unlucky and see the other guy make a set, that's just part of poker. Bad things can happen to good hands.

If an opponent calls your raise with A-K, A-Q, or A-J, they are in a heap of trouble, right where you want them. This is why I prefer raising with pocket aces. If an opponent plays back at you, you have the chance to win a big pot. If you raise and he reraises preflop, you have to decide whether you want to come over the top or slowplay your aces. In other words, do you want to shut him out right there or do you want to play the pot with him? A lot of times, I'll play him a pot. But if I get reraised and a third player calls the reraise, I'll move in—I don't necessarily want to play against two opponents, I want to win the pot right there or at least get heads-up.

## Setting the Standard Raise

Every time the limit increases in no-limit tournaments, the first player that puts in a raise generally sets the standard for the amount that everybody else is going to raise during that level. For example, if the first raise is $300, that becomes the standard raise that everyone makes. But when I play, I try to break the standard. If the going rate is $300, I might make my standard raise $400. I want to be called, so every time I raise I put in my standard amount, not theirs.

A lot of tournament players vary their bets depending on the value of their cards—which means that you can tell what they have by how much they wager. Often, they'll make a smaller raise with aces than they ordinarily would because they want to get played with. Many limit hold'em players who are new to no-limit hold'em move all in with two aces, trying to win the antes. Neither play makes sense—the whole idea of poker is to get as much value as you can get from your hands, and neither play helps you do that.

I don't vary the size of my raises because I don't want to tip the strength of my hand. Obviously the amount of the raise will differ at each level of the tournament, because as you get deeper the blinds are higher and there's more money involved.

But the point is that if you raise $400 with A-K, also raise $400 with two aces or two kings, for example.

---

**KEY CONCEPT**

Don't tip the strength of your hand by varying the amount of your raises.

---

Now let's look at three scenarios that demonstrate how you might play pocket aces from early position when you are the first player in the pot.

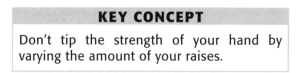

## Slow Playing A-A in Early Position

You are sitting in early position and have been dealt A-A. You limp into the pot. The player in the cutoff seat raises. The button and both of the blinds fold. You decide to just call his raise. The flop comes:

### YOUR HAND

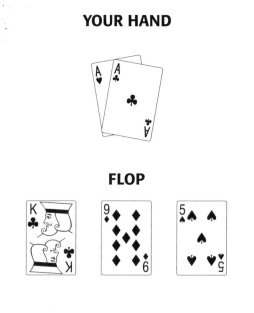

### FLOP

Now what do you do? Since you have set things up to slowplay your hand, you check. Your opponent bets. You flat call. The turn card is the 2♠.

You check. The preflop raiser puts in a big bet. You raise, knowing that there's a good chance that you'll get played with if he has something such as A-K or a pocket pair such as queens or jacks. Your opponent calls. The river comes with another deuce. You bet. He calls and turns over the A♠ K♠.

**YOU**                    **OPPONENT**

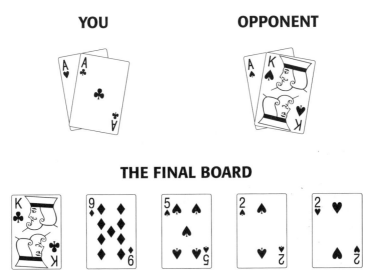

**THE FINAL BOARD**

Your opponent had top pair with the nut flush draw on the turn. Because you limped before the flop and checked to him on the flop, he probably thought that he had the best hand by a long shot, or a tie at the very least. He didn't put you on a set, and it wouldn't even occur to most players that you might have pocket aces.

This is the perfect scenario for slowplaying pocket aces and getting full value—and it's one way to trap your opponent. Now let's look at a different style of slowplaying aces from early position.

## ACTION HAND 3
### Raising with A-A in Early Position

You are Player A and have been dealt the A♣ A♦. This time you raise from early position with your pocket aces. Player B reraises, and you flat call. The board comes the same as last time.

### YOUR HAND

### THE FINAL BOARD

When the flop comes K-9-5, you are thinking, "How can I get the most out of this pot?" If you lead at the pot, Player B probably will raise if he has A-K. You don't want him to fold, so you don't make a huge bet. Instead, you bet an amount that you believe he will call if he has any kind of hand. Whether he calls or raises, you have him trapped—unless he has pocket kings, in which case you're the one who is trapped.

You lead at the pot all the way through. Why? Because his preflop reraise and his call on the flop tell you that he is pot-committed. In this situation, your preflop raise built a decent pot for you to win.

## *ACTION HAND 4*

### Getting Reraised with A-A

You are Player A. You raise from early position with A♣ A♥. Player B reraises, and Player C cold calls the reraise. Now what do you do?

In this situation, you know that Player C has a big hand, probably K-K or Q-Q, so you go over the top with an all-in bet. There's enough money in the pot already to make it worth winning, so you move on it. You hope for a call, but even if both Players B and C fold, you still have won a decent pot.

Now suppose you reraise Player C's raise, Player B folds, and Player C calls your reraise. The flop comes the same as it did before.

**YOUR HAND**

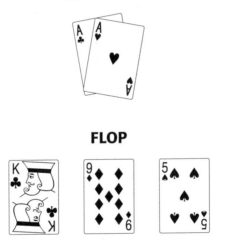

**FLOP**

At this point you have two options: Either lead at it all the way, or just move in on the flop. You want to get paid off on your aces, but even if you move all-in on the flop and Player C does not call, you've still won a big pot with your aggressive play of pocket aces from up front.

# WHEN YOU HAVE A-A IN MIDDLE POSITION

If the pot has been opened or raised in the first three seats, you have two options with pocket aces—you can play "second-hand low," or you can raise. Here's how second-hand low works.

Suppose you're in a real action game. A player in early position limps in front of you. Instead of raising, you limp in with A♣ A♦. Two other players also limp behind you. Then an opponent who has been raising every pot puts in a raise. You anticipated that he would raise against two or more limpers, so you set the raiser up in advance to play second-hand low.

## Playing Second-Hand Low: Setting the Trap

You know that a real action player is sitting behind you, so when an opponent leads into the pot in front of you, you just call. You suspect that the original limper might also have a big hand, so you're setting the stage to raise both the limper and the action player. You are playing second-hand low. Your goal is to trap everybody, and make them pay to try to draw out on your aces.

The first player in the pot probably has a decent hand, but you have pocket aces, the best starting hand in no-limit hold'em. The first player might reraise the pot after the loose player raises, giving you the chance to win a big pot before the flop by coming over the top. If you reraise right there, your opponents might figure that you're just trying to pick up the pot, or that you have A-K or something like that. Opponents hardly ever put you on pocket aces when you play second-hand low because you just called the opener's bet to start with.

Even if the first player in the pot brings it in for a raise, you still play second-hand low by just flat calling his raise in the hope that someone behind you (most likely the action player) will reraise. If that doesn't happen, there's still a chance that the player who raised up front will come after you on the flop.

> ## KEY CONCEPT
>
> When you play second-hand low, opponents hardly ever put you on pocket aces because you just called the opener's preflop bet.

In fact, if you have several action players in the game, you can even play third-hand low if all of the action players are sitting behind you. You can be the third limper. You can pull it off even if the pot has been raised and called in front of you, in which case you can also flat call with the intention of reraising if one of the action players raises behind you. Naturally, you have to know your opponents very well to pull off this play.

Now let's look at a scenario in which you raise preflop from middle position with A-A and compare it with a scenario in which you play second-hand low.

## ACTION HAND 5

### Raising with A-A in Middle Position

You are in middle position with the A♣ A♠. You raised the pot before the flop. Player B called on the button and Player C called in the big blind. The flop comes:

### YOUR HAND

### FLOP

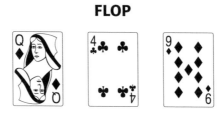

You make a standard bet in the hope of getting called by someone holding A-Q, K-Q, Q-J, Q-10, a 9 with a big kicker, a J-10 (straight draw), or someone with a diamond draw. You could get beaten by these drawing hands or by any hand that makes two pair. But in all of these scenarios, you're still the favorite on the flop. The only drawing hand that is better off than your aces is J♦ 10♦, and even that hand is only a slight favorite on this flop.

The fourth street card is the 5♥. You must bet enough on the turn to put pressure on your opponents. You want to force them to decide whether they want to commit a lot of money to this pot. Obviously you are a good favorite over all the hands mentioned. The 2♥ comes on the river.

## YOUR HAND

## THE FINAL BOARD

If anyone has stayed in the hand to the river, I would empty out (bet all my chips) hoping to get called. The way that the hand has been played should indicate that A-A is still the best hand. In this scenario, I did not forget about the possibility that somebody flopped a set, but because of the straight and flush possibilities on board, I am sure that if anyone had flopped a set, he would have moved on the flop, or certainly on fourth street.

Now look at how you might play A-A using the second-hand-low strategy.

## *ACTION HAND 6*

### Playing Second-Hand Low with A-A

Before the flop, one player limps into the pot from an early position. You know from his previous play that he could be holding anything. You are next to act. Your hand is the A♣ A♦. You decide to just call. The button, the small blind, and the big blind also flat call. The flop comes:

### YOUR HAND

### FLOP

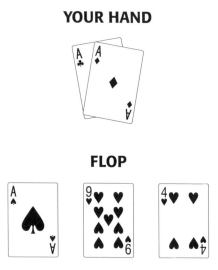

The two blinds and the early limper check. You also check. The button bets, the two blinds fold, and the original limper calls. Obviously you don't know exactly what the button and the limper have, but you do know that you have the best possible hand. You have two choices for playing the hand.

Knowing that you have disguised the strength of your hand, do you flat call in the hope of winning a huge pot on fourth or fifth street? Or do you raise the pot on the flop so as not to give any free cards? Let's take a look at two possible scenarios.

### Action Choice A: Flat Call on the Flop

Along with the early-position limper, you flat called the button's bet on the flop. The turn card is the 10♣.

### YOUR HAND

### TURN

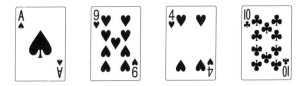

Now you have them where you want them! It's time to get the most value from your hand. If the limper checks, lead at the pot with a decent bet, hoping that one or both of your opponents will either raise or call. If either player raises, he has committed himself to the pot. In that case, you go on the offensive and move all-in. You know that there is a very good chance that at least one of them is on a big draw, has flopped a set, or has made top two pair. Suppose one of them calls your all-in bet and the river is the 5♠.

## YOUR HAND

## THE FINAL BOARD

How sweet it is!

But what if either or both opponents flat call on the turn? In that case, on the river when you know that you have the nuts, bet the amount that you think they will call. You don't move in because you don't want them to throw their hands away, you simply want to get full value from your aces. The difference between good and average players is that a good player always does whatever it takes to get full value from a hand.

### Action Choice B: Raise on the Flop

Now suppose that you choose to raise the pot right on the flop so as not to give any free cards, but still with the hope that either or both opponents will call. Understand that if either opponent calls the raise, his hand would have to be a set, top two pair, top and bottom pair, A-K or A-Q, a flush draw, or a pair with a flush draw. If either opponent has a pair and a flush draw, he would have to have an ace and a flush draw.

Let's say that both the limper and the button call your raise. Again, the board looks like this on fourth street:

## YOUR HAND

## TURN

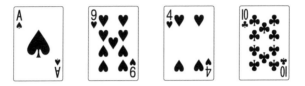

The limper checks. What do you do? You make a big bet, looking to either win the pot right there or get called by one or both opponents. Suppose the button calls and the limper folds. Again the 5♠ comes on the river.

This time you are the first to act—what do you do? It's time for the kill! You've put him on a big hand and now you want to find out just how important it is to him, so you shove in all your chips. Does life get much sweeter than this?

### The Hands at the Showdown

**YOUR HAND**  **OPPONENT A**  **OPPONENT B**

**THE FINAL BOARD**

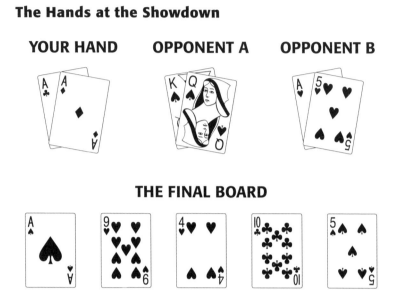

After the hand is over, you discover that the limper had the K♠ Q♠ and the button had the A♥ 5♥. The button probably stayed to the river because he put you on a flush draw. Then when he paired his kicker, he expected his two pair (aces and fives) to win a big pot for him.

# WHEN YOU HAVE A-A IN LATE POSITION

Suppose you have been dealt A♠ A♣ in the cutoff seat. How do you play your hand? It doesn't matter how many people are in the pot—you should raise, period. After everyone has passed to the button, you sometimes will see a player limp with pocket aces, but I think that's a horrible play. Always raise with aces from a late position. The chances of someone raising from the two blinds are slim, since you have two of the four aces in the deck locked up. And if they don't raise, they're going to get free cards on the flop with any kind of hand, in which case you will have no idea of where you are on the flop with your aces.

If someone has raised in front of you with a lot of players in the pot, you need to reraise. You cannot give free cards very often in a tournament if you want to survive. A lot of times your opponents will discount the strength of a late-position raise and will play with you because they believe you're on a steal.

Make your standard raise if you're the first one in the pot, or if there's only one limper in front of you. However, if more than one player is already in, you should consider pushing all your chips to the center of the table. Any time you have pocket aces, you want someone to come over the top of you. When an opponent does that, your only decision is whether to just flat call and try to nail him after the flop, or move in immediately to try to win the pot right there. Of course, if you flat call, there's always the danger that your opponent will outflop you. But when you're playing pocket aces in no-limit poker, you should always choose the bolder strategy to try to get as much value out of the hand as possible.

# WHEN YOU HAVE A-A IN THE BLINDS

When you have aces in one of the blinds, it is more important to raise than it is in any other position. Why? Because you always have to act first after the flop. You are in the weakest position at the start of the hand, so you need to play aces right, which means raising.

Suppose everybody checks to the button. He raises and the small blind folds. You're sitting in the big blind with the

A♣ A♠. In this situation you might try to trap the button by just flat calling the raise in the hope that something will come on the flop that hits him a little bit but hits you even better. The best scenario you can hope for is that your opponent has something like A-6.

## ACTION HAND 7

### Playing Aces Heads Up at the WSOP

Pocket aces is such a powerful hand that you raise with them most of the time from any position, period. Take a look at this example from the WSOP to see what sometimes happens when you limp with aces. In the last hand of the championship match in 2001, Dewey Tomko and Carlos Mortensen were heads-up at the final table. Dewey limped with two aces on the button—which is the small blind in heads-up play—and Carlos raised $70,000 with the K♣ Q♣. Dewey decided to just flat call.

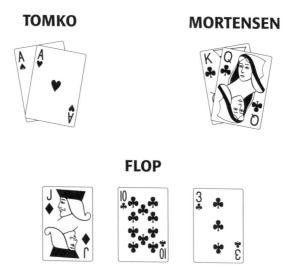

TOMKO　　　　　MORTENSEN

FLOP

Carlos would have been a slight favorite on the flop—if Dewey hadn't had two aces. But since Dewey had two of the aces that Carlos needed to make a straight, Carlos was a slight dog with two cards to come. He had 26 wins (13 outs twice)—a 9, an ace, any club, or runner-runner to beat two aces. Against any other hand except pocket aces Carlos would have had 30 outs. He even would've had 30 outs against a set, but not against aces since they were two of his win cards. If Dewey had had two jacks in the hole, Carlos would have had more outs than he had against the aces.

Carlos bet $100,000 on the flop and Dewey raised $400,000. Carlos reraised without hesitation, moving in all his chips. Dewey called—all the money was sitting in the middle on the flop. It came down to two aces against a double draw for a flush or straight. So, what happened? The drawing hand won when the 9♦ came on the river, giving Carlos a straight and the World Championship of Poker.

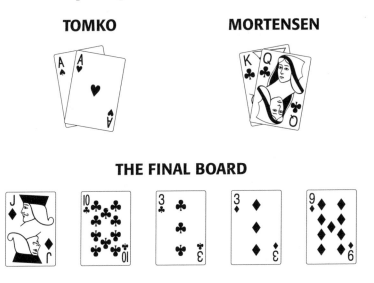

## TOMKO          MORTENSEN

## THE FINAL BOARD

Nothing was wrong with Dewey's slowplay of the aces—he got the action he wanted from Carlos. But Carlos got the type of flop he needed and Dewey's pocket rockets went down in flames.

# WHEN BAD THINGS HAPPEN TO GOOD HANDS

Believe me, I know how Dewey felt. Been there, done that! I was playing in the Legends of Poker tournament at the Bicycle Club, when I caught two red aces in the little blind. John Hom raised the pot, and the button moved all in. Holding the best hand in poker, naturally I called all-in. Hom had more money than me, and knowing that I wouldn't go all-in without a huge hand, he laid down his two black kings. It was heads-up between me and the button, who had A-K offsuit.

I had a huge percentage of the deck in my favor. However, something bad happened to my good hand. The board finished with four spades. The button won it with the A♠ and knocked me out of the tournament. Hom had thrown away the K♠, so even he could have beaten my aces with a king-high flush!

And that isn't the only time I've been beaten with A-A. At the no-limit championship event at the Bike one year, Phil Hellmuth had just bluffed at me and I had doubled up with two pair. On the next hand, I looked down to see A-A, so I brought it in for the standard raise. Phil was in the big blind and I knew that he was hot as hell because he had just doubled me up. Sure enough, when it got to him he said, "All in!" and bet $6,400 more. I called. He had A-Q offsuit against my two aces. The board came K-10-4-J-x, and I was out of that tournament. Amazing! But that's aces for you.

# PLAYING ACES IN THE LATE STAGE

These hands from major tournament action occurred near the end of play. Here are some tips on how you might play pocket aces in the late stages of a tournament. Suppose you have A-A and somebody has raised in front of you. What's your best play? You must decide whether you want to move all-in, or just reraise an amount that you think he will call so that you can get him to pay you off later in the hand. Say that you reraised and the board comes 9 high. Is he the type of player who will lead at the pot with J-J in the hole? Think about these things before you reraise.

A good player always tries to extract as much money as he can from a hand. If your opponent is a really good player, you might as well just move him in and see if he wants to play with you. If he's an average player, you may want to reraise an amount that you think he will call. If you've put him on a decent pocket pair, you hope for a small flop so that you can pick up the rest of his chips. Again, you play each type of player differently.

---

### KEY CONCEPT

A good player always extracts as much money as he can from a hand.

---

# WINNING WITH BIG POCKET PAIRS

You're always happy to be dealt a big pocket pair in a tournament, the higher the better. But it's how you play them that determines how happy you'll be at the end of the day. This chapter gives you pointers on how to play kings, queens and jacks. Let's start off with K-K, the second-best pair you can be dealt—and the most dangerous. To find out why, read on.

## HOW TO PLAY POCKET KINGS

Pocket kings is a very difficult hand to get away from before the flop—and that is why it's such a treacherous hand in tournament poker. This is not to say that K-K is an unplayable hand—it's a great hand. It's just that you have to be careful not to get so excited about being dealt cowboys that you hang onto them for too long and wind up losing money to them.

If an opponent raises in front of you before the flop, you usually reraise with K-K to limit the field. You'd be okay with winning it right there, but there's always the chance that you will run into A-A, or a big ace (A-K), or even "any ace" (A-7). And if somebody calls you with an ace in his hand, you're a goner if an ace comes on the flop.

Any time the pot is raised and reraised in front of you on the flop in a tournament, I suggest that you dump your two kings. Even if it means losing a winnable pot once in a while, you will save a lot of money in the long run.

One of the most famous laydowns in tournament history occurred at the inaugural Tournament of Champions of Poker that Mike Sexton founded. In heads-up play at the final table, David Chiu folded pocket kings against Louis Asmo's all-in bet. Louis had made it known that he really wanted to win the tournament and wouldn't do anything to jeopardize his chances, and everybody knew it. In fact, he has playing his A-game.

Knowing how strongly Asmo felt about winning, Chiu realized that the only hand he could be holding when he went all-in was pocket aces. And that is why he laid down the kings. Asmo graciously showed his aces as soon as Chiu folded. As it turned out, Chiu's smart decision led him to victory in the tournament.

Now let's look at a couple of situations in which you have been dealt K-K.

# WHEN YOU HAVE K-K IN EARLY POSITION

Suppose you are playing in the middle stage of a $1,000 no-limit tournament. You look down to find the K♣ K♥. You are Player A, the first to act. How do you play the hand before the flop?

### Action Choice One

You might limp with K-K from front position, hoping that someone will raise. If somebody behind you has A-A, more power to him—there's nothing you can do about it. The strategy behind limping with kings is to let somebody raise you so that you can reraise and win the pot immediately. If a player just calls, you still have the second-best hand that you can start with. You just hope that an ace doesn't come on the board. Two kings are so hard to play because it seems that an ace so often comes on the flop when you have them.

## Action Choice Two

Say that you limp with the kings from an early position, Player B raises, Player C calls the raise, and you reraise. More likely than not, you will win the pot right there, unless either Player B or C has A-A. If either one of them reraises, you're probably a gone goose. If Player B has aces, for example, he will move you all-in. If he doesn't move in, there's a pretty good chance that you have the best hand. If Player C reraises, he would have to be a very good player to check-raise in this situation with A-A. It takes a superior player to pull off this play, and you don't see it very often in tournaments. Therefore, it is unlikely that Player C has A-A.

## ACTION HAND 8

### Playing K-K on a Rag Flop

How you play pocket kings against a rag flop depends on what you know about your opponents. This example from the WSOP illustrates how knowledge of your opponents can save you a lot of misery in tournament poker.

Let's take a look at a hand that came up during the first level of play at a $10,000 World Series of Poker championship event. I picked up the K♦ K♠ and made it $300 to go. Jay Heimowitz called. The flop came:

 **T.J.**   **JAY**

## FLOP

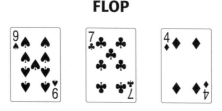

I bet $400 at the pot and Jay made a big raise of around $3,000. I didn't hesitate in throwing away the kings because I knew that he wouldn't raise me with anything smaller than two aces or a set. Sure enough, he showed me the 9♣ 9♥.

If I had been playing Joe Blow from Idaho, I might have given him a little action on this hand, especially if I knew that he was a limit hold'em player making a transition to no-limit. Limit players seem to think that when they have top pair with top kicker or an overpair in no-limit hold'em, they have the Holy City.

Jay is an excellent player, so I knew that he would not have stood a raise with a hand such as A-J, so he had to have a pocket pair. The only pairs that I could have beaten on the flop were tens, jacks, or queens. When you're playing against a top player like Jay, he isn't moving in with two jacks, two queens, or even two kings. So, I figured that he either had two aces or a set—he wouldn't have 10-8 or 8-6 for a straight draw. I lost $700 on the hand, but at least I wasn't knocked out of the tournament.

A player such as Heimowitz knows that I either have an overpair or am taking a shot with A-K or A-Q (since it was a small flop), and that I am putting him on either the A-K or A-Q, too. But once I bet the flop and he raised it, I knew where he was at with the hand.

Why did he make such a huge raise? If he put me on a big overpair, he may have figured that I would play it, but I didn't. He also knew that if he flat called I would shut down if I didn't hit anything, so he may as well try to get me to play the hand on the flop. Jay realized that he had the pot won on the flop, so why not take it right then? Why give me a chance to bust him if one of my cards came off on the turn? You never want to give a free card in a tournament.

Actually, this was the second time in a row that Jay flopped top set against an overpair. On the hand just before this one, Tommy Grimes had A-A and brought it in for about $400. Jay called the bet. The flop came 10-7-2. Tommy bet $2,000 at the pot and Jay moved in. Tommy made the mistake of calling him. Jay had 10-10 and flopped top set, knocking Tommy out of the tournament.

---

### KEY CONCEPT

Knowing your opponents can save you lots of misery.

---

## ACTION HAND 9

### Playing Kings on an Ace-High Board

I hear so many players say, "Every time I have kings, an ace comes on the flop." If an ace shows up, so what? If you think your opponent has an ace in his hand, just fold.

### Action Choice One

Suppose you are holding the K♣ K♠ in the middle stage of a $1,000 buy-in tournament. Player A has limped into the pot. You raise, everyone else folds, and the limper calls. The flop comes:

## YOUR HAND

## FLOP

Player A checks. What do you do? A lot of players will check their ace on the flop, especially with a weak kicker. You should also check.

### Action Choice Two

You are in first position with the K♠ K♦. You raised before the flop and Player B called your raise. What do you do when the flop comes with an ace?

Because the ace is on the board, you check. Player B probably also checks—a good player will check his ace on the flop if the raiser has checked in front of him. Suppose the turn comes with the 2♣. Now what? In tournament play, you check again.

## YOUR HAND

## TURN

Player B probably will bet, although he could wait until fifth street. He knows that you don't have an ace and he may try to trap you on the end. But once the ace comes on the flop, you are through with the hand. You will only play it to the showdown if you can play it for free.

## *ACTION HAND 10*

### Playing K-K as an Overpair

In the middle stage of a big no-limit tournament, you are dealt two kings for the third time. You raise before the flop and one opponent calls. The flop comes:

### YOUR HAND

### FLOP

How do you play your overpair on the flop?

This time, you lead with the kings, thinking that someone at the table holds a hand such as A♠ Q♦ or K♥ Q♥, which are hands that a player might call a raise with. If one of those hands is out, then you might get a play when you bet. If a blank comes on the turn, you want to make a healthy bet because you don't want to give anybody a chance to make two pair on the river.

But what if you're up against a player who stood your preflop raise with Q-Q? Some tournament players think that queens are the holy nuts and will even reraise with them preflop. But since nobody reraised you before the flop, you go with the kings and then try to shut out your opponents on fourth street with a big bet.

There's also the chance that someone holds K-J suited and will call your opening bet on a straight draw. Although he probably will call you on the flop, he will throw away the hand if you put in a big bet at fourth street, unless he is a horrible player. In no-limit or pot-limit hold'em, you can freeze out the draws on the turn, whereas in limit hold'em you can't.

## ACTION HAND 11

### Playing K-K at the WSOP

Hans "Tuna" Lund and I were faced with this hand one year at the World Series of Poker. Tuna raised the pot from early position and it was passed all the way to me on the button. I flat called him with the K♠ K♣. The flop came:

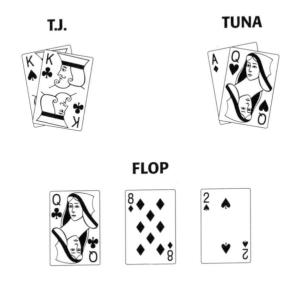

**T.J.**

**TUNA**

**FLOP**

Tuna led at the pot with his top pair/top kicker. What would you do in my situation?

I flat called the bet. On the turn, he led at the pot again. This time, I moved over the top of him. And what did Tuna do? He tossed his hand into the muck.

In this example, I played to win a big pot and was able to extract $2,700 from my opponent. I knew that Tuna likely held A-Q or A-K before the flop, but there was a pretty good chance that I had the best hand, as K-K is the second-best pair you can be dealt. It pays to take a chance once in a while.

# HOW TO PLAY POCKET QUEENS

Two queens can be very difficult to play in both no-limit and pot-limit hold'em. It's almost always too good to throw away, but it's also vulnerable against A-K, as well as K-K and A-A. Often, your success in a tournament depends on when you push with queens and when you get away from them, or when you do both.

I was playing at the Bellagio Five-Diamond tournament and faced this situation. The first spot brought it in for a raise of $150. Four players called before it got to me in the little blind. Looking down at the Q♦ Q♣, I reraised $1,200. I overbet the pot a little bit because I wanted to win it right there, or at least see only one other player call me. The big blind called the $1,200 and raised another $4,000.

Everybody folded around to me. I threw the queens away so fast they looked like 3-2. The big blind showed me K-K, but that's beside the point. The point is that if you're not prepared to get away from two queens, you'd better not play no-limit hold'em. Although there are many scenarios where Q-Q is a great hand, there also are a lot of situations where it isn't.

---

### KEY CONCEPT

If you're not prepared to fold pocket queens, you'd better not play no-limit hold'em.

---

## Two Ways Not to Play Q-Q

Do not slowplay queens from a front position because any ace or king that comes on the flop will put you in jeopardy. You want to bring them in for a raise in order to get some money into the pot. In the early stage of the tournament, if a player reraises a substantial portion of his chips before the flop, pocket queens is not the type of hand that you want to take a stand with. You cannot afford to take any heat with before the flop. You should release them in this scenario. A smart, timely laydown is just as important as making the right calls and raises.

Further, you should not play pocket queens second-hand low. Why? Because when you just call after a couple of limpers have entered the pot, you don't know where you're at with pocket queens. Pocket aces is the only hand that you play second-hand low strategy.

## ACTION HAND 12

### Playing Q-Q in Early Position

Suppose you raise preflop from an early position with pocket queens in early position. Only one opponent calls your raise, so you play the flop heads-up. The flop comes:

### YOUR HAND

### FLOP

What do you do against this type of flop?

You bet. You can beat A-J, Q-J, 10-9, and other hands like them. If you check, you face the possibility that an ace or king will come on the turn and you will lose a hand that you should have won.

If your opponent has 10-9 for a straight draw, he likely will call you on the flop, but your bet will force him to pay if he wants to see the turn card. Of course, it's also possible that he is slowplaying with A-A or K-K or even 8-8. But still, you can't afford to give a free card when you have pocket queens.

The only time that you can trap with queens is when you're up against very aggressive players who will bet every time you check. But overall, never give a free card in tournament poker when you have what appears to be the best hand on the flop.

## ACTION HAND 13

### Playing Q-Q in Late Position

Pocket queens gain more value if you hold them in late position or, more importantly, on the button, and some players have limped in front of you. In that case, the chances are that no one behind you in the blinds has a bigger pair than yours. Always raise with the queens in this situation. And if you get a small flop, you can try to win the pot right away.

For example, suppose you raised preflop and two players called your raise. The flop comes:

### YOUR HAND

### FLOP

Both of your opponents check to you. Here's your chance to make a decent bet and take down the good-sized pot you created by raising before the flop.

> ### KEY CONCEPT
>
> It's not how you play pocket queens when you have the best hand that counts the most—it's how well you get away from them when you don't.

Although it sounds as though we're telling you to play pocket queens very cautiously, Q-Q is actually the third-best starting hand in hold'em. They increase in value as the number of players at your tournament table decreases. Just keep in mind that the lower your big pair, the more big pairs that are higher, and the more overcards that can beat you. The major consideration with queens is not what you do with them when you have the best hand, but how you get away from them when you don't.

# HOW TO PLAY POCKET JACKS

The way you play pocket jacks is heavily dependent upon your position at the table. Let's take a look at several scenarios to understand the difference.

## When You Have J-J in Early Position

Suppose you are sitting in a front position during the early stage of a no-limit tournament. You look down to find J♠ J♦ in the hole. The player under the gun folds and you are next to act. Do you bring it in with a raise, or do you just limp?

My suggestion is that you limp with J-J (or 10-10) in this situation. If you raise and get reraised, what are you going to do with the hand? If you don't get raised, you could flop a jack and win a big pot, because nobody will put you on such a good hand to start with. You take the chance, of course, that a player will come in with something like an A-9 or K-Q and beat you.

If someone outflops you and wins the hand, you would have been beaten anyway. But by not raising before the flop, you will lose less money if somebody does make a better hand on the flop.

Of course, if you had raised with your jacks before the flop, they may not have played those ace-small or K-Q hands. But your bigger worry is getting reraised and being forced to throw away the hand when you have money invested in the pot.

## When You Have J-J in Middle Position

Suppose you are sitting in fifth position and everyone has passed to you. In that case, you should raise with J-J at any point in the tournament. This situation is very different from scenario one, as now you already have four people out of the pot and there are only four players sitting behind you.

Early in the tournament when the antes are $25/$50, you might raise $150 to $200 with J-J. In big buy-in tournaments such as the WSOP or WPT, you start with $10,000, so $200 would be a reasonable raise. Don't make huge raises of $4,000, for example, early in a tournament. Instead, make a small raise because you think that you have the best hand before the flop. You are trying to do one of two things: Either win the pot immediately, or get called and win the pot as it develops. After all, J-J is not the best hand that you can have; in fact, you cannot even call with the hand on a lot of flops.

## Playing J-J in the Late Stage

When you're playing in the late stages of a tournament with J-J in the hole, you definitely want to raise. Say that you are playing at a short-handed table with six or fewer players. Four tables are left in the tournament and each one of them is short-handed. In that case you have to play the jacks much stronger than you would earlier in the event, although you don't necessarily want to commit your whole stack with the jacks.

Now, let's turn to one of the best hands you can be dealt in tournament poker, A-K. There are pluses and minuses to Big Slick, which we'll discuss in detail in the next chapter.

# WINNING WITH ACE-KING

Big Slick is the biggest "decision" hand in tournament play. To win a no-limit hold'em tournament, you have to win when you have A-K and you have to win when you're up against A-K. Although it may not happen on the final hand, A-K often will be the *deciding* hand, the one with which you win or lose the most chips.

Let's take a look at several tournament scenarios and analyze how to play A-K according to the situation.

## *ACTION HAND 14*

### Playing A-K in Middle Position

At a no-limit tournament table, Player A raises $1,200 before the flop. You are Player B and reraise $1,200 with the A♣ K♠. Player C cold calls your reraise, and so does Player A. The flop comes:

### YOUR HAND

### FLOP

### Situation One

Player A bets $8,000 on the flop. As Player B, what is your best move?

If I were you (Player B), I would have just flat called Player A's $1,200 raise before the flop. Why? Because I want to see what comes on the flop to help me decide how strong to play my hand. Or I would've reraised about four times that amount if I had enough chips. My reraise would have been big enough to shut out the rest of the field so that I could play heads-up against one opponent. If you make a large raise, the original raiser might throw his hand away and you will win the pot right there, or maybe he'll call. In either case, your raise probably will freeze out the rest of the field.

But you didn't do either of these things. You allowed Player C to come into the pot—the guy even cold called your raise—so you have to give both Player A and Player C credit for having good hands.

When Player A bets $8,000 on the flop, what is your best move? I would fold at this point. First of all, Player A has either A-A, A-K, Q-Q, A-Q, or possibly 7-7 if he's a loose player. Since I am holding the K♠, I don't put him on a spade draw. Secondly, since Player C cold called behind me preflop, he also could have flopped a set. After this analysis of my opponents' possible hands, I would fold the A-K.

## Situation Two

Player A checks on the flop. What's your best move? You should also check.

## Situation Three

Player A moves all-in on the flop. What's your best move? You should fold.

Some of the key elements you need to know to make an accurate analysis are missing from this situation—for example, how many players are at the table; whether this hand comes up in the early, middle, or late stage of the tournament; and what you know about your opponents. You should know which players will raise or reraise with A-J or A-Q, and who won't raise unless they have A-A or K-K—because you have been studying them. If your opponent is the type that will not raise with a weak hand, you don't have anything with the A-K, so why not get rid of it?

## Situation Four

Suppose you have $2,500 in front of you. You bring it in for $1,500, and somebody reraises behind you. What's your move?

You are pot-committed. You have more than one-half of your chips already in the pot, so you go on with the hand. An experienced player often will pot-commit by putting in most of his chips when he raises because he knows that if he gets reraised, he will automatically go for the rest of it. Less experienced players sometimes think they can blow the raiser off the hand by reraising—that the raiser will save that extra $500 or $1,000 that he has left. What an inexperienced reraiser doesn't realize is that the only reason the original raiser has committed himself to the pot is so that he can't get away from the hand. He wants to see it all the way through the river.

---

### KEY CONCEPT

To win a no-limit hold'em tournament, you have to win when you have A-K and you have to win when you're up against A-K.

---

## ACTION HAND 15

### Playing A-K in a Big Pot on a Huge Flop

You are playing at a full table during the middle stage of a $1,000 buy-in tournament. Player A raises $1,200 before the flop. You are Player B, sitting in fifth position with four players behind you. Holding the A♣ K♠, you reraise $4,800. Player C cold calls your reraise, shoving in $6,000 ($1,200 plus $4,800). Player A also calls, making a big pot. The flop comes:

## YOUR HAND

## FLOP

### Situation One

Player A checks on the flop, putting you in a quandary. You have top pair/top kicker and the nut flush draw, and there is $18,000 in the pot. This could be the perfect trap hand, but you have to play it, so you move in with all of your chips. You can't beat a set, of course, but you're still drawing to the nut flush. It doesn't matter what Player C does—you're going to play the hand anyway.

### Situation Two

Player A bets. What do you do? Again, you move all-in. You can't hope for a better flop, unless it had come A-A-K. This is a flop that you have to play.

## ACTION HAND 16

### Playing A-K on a Tricky Flop

Once again, you have been dealt Big Slick. The tournament conditions and preflop action are the same as they were in the previous example. This time the flop comes:

## YOUR HAND

## FLOP

### Situation One

Player A bets. You know he's a pretty good player because you've been carefully observing his play. You fold your A-K.

Why? Because a lot of times, good players will make a move with a big hand, trying to induce you into playing back at them. Since it's clear that Player A knows what he's doing, you should throw the hand away.

### Situation Two

Player A checks. What is your best move? You also check. What if Player C bets after both of you check to him? You fold. Tossing your hand is tough to do because you have a lot of money in the pot. But why give up the tournament for one hand? The A-K is a perfect trap hand, unless you're playing at a short-handed table where it is more powerful.

If you're playing against five or fewer players, A-K is quite strong, but if you're in a full ring, there are a lot of scenarios when Big Slick amounts to nothing. You want to avoid as many traps as possible in tournament poker.

Given this flop, there is a good chance that either Player A or C has flopped quad queens, or a full house if either one is holding an A-Q. Pocket queens is a decent raising hand, one that a lot of players will stand a reraise with (although I'm not one of them). People think that Big Slick is a big-big hand, but it isn't—in fact, two deuces is a better hand heads-up than A-K. In a computer run of 100,000 hands, two deuces will win more often than A-K in heads-up situations played to a showdown.

## ACTION HAND 17

### Playing A-K on a Baby Flop

You have Big Slick in middle position. Again Player A raises, you reraise, and Player C cold calls. Player A also calls, so the three of you are in action when the flop comes out with three baby cards.

**YOUR HAND**

**FLOP**

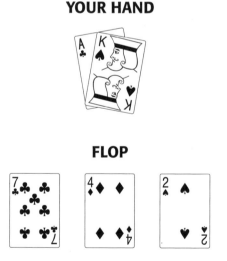

## Situation One

Player A bets. What's your move? You throw your hand away. Why? Because you have nothing. In no-limit hold'em, you never chase.

## Situation Two

Player A checks. What do you do? You also check.

## Situation Three

Player A checks, you check, and player C bets. Now what? You fold, no matter what Player A does in front of you after Player C bets. Again, you never chase with A-K in no-limit hold'em.

Remember that Player C cold called a reraise before the flop and gets to act after you. It's fairly certain that he can beat a pair of deuces, fours or sevens, and your A-K can't beat any of those pairs. So, that's another reason why you dump your A-K if he bets.

---

### KEY CONCEPT

Big Slick is a drawing hand before the flop.

---

Of all the connected hands, A-K has the highest two connectors you can be dealt, and can win a pot on its strength alone with no help from the board. Just keep in mind that A-K is still a drawing hand, as we have emphasized in all our books. In the next chapter, we illustrate how to play other big connectors in no-limit hold'em tournaments.

# WINNING WITH BIG CONNECTORS

It is not unusual for players to raise from early position with A-K, A-Q, A-J, or A-10 in no-limit hold'em tournaments. However, when you're playing at a full table, I think that hands such as A-Q, A-J, or A-10 (suited or unsuited) in the first four seats are very weak. Why? Because if you raise with them and get called, where are you? And if you get raised, it's hard to justify continuing with the hand. It seems that when you start with the worst hand, you invariably flop a pair to it and then you're stuck in the pot. Always try to avoid that situation by not playing these types of hands in early position, especially in a no-limit hold'em tournament.

## HOW TO PLAY A-Q

Ace-queen is a trouble hand that you need to play cautiously. During the first levels of play in a nine- or ten-handed game you don't want to put a lot of money in the pot with A-Q (suited or unsuited) from an early position. Treat a suited hand as a bonus, but something that should not change how you play. Although I prefer suited cards when I play an A-Q, A-J, or A-10, I value their ranks more than whether or not they're suited.

You can't stand a reraise before the flop with A-Q in the opening rounds. If you catch either an ace or a queen on the flop, you will be in a bind as to what to do if someone bets at you. Why put yourself in that situation?

Suppose you flop a queen and an early position raiser makes a big bet at the pot. Ask yourself what he could have, particularly if he's willing to jeopardize a lot of his chips. People won't usually risk going broke early in a tournament unless they have a big pocket pair. In fact, it's easier to play *any* pair from up front than A-Q because small to medium pairs play so easily after the flop—no set, no bet—whereas an A-Q or A-J require a lot of judgment if you get any action on the flop.

If I'm in middle to late position early in the tournament and there are other limpers in the pot, I'll consider taking a cheap flop with the hand, but I won't raise with it. If there are no limpers, I like to bring it for a modest raise of about three times the size of the big blind. If anyone comes over the top I fold. If I flop top pair, I usually will make a pot-sized bet on the flop, but if I get played with, I usually will shut down.

Later in the tournament, particularly when you're playing at a short-handed table, A-Q becomes more valuable. Although I don't suggest raising with A-Q in a full ring, I will raise with the hand when the table is five-handed or less. When you're either short stacked or are up against a short stack, you might have to take a stand with the hand.

Now, let's take a look at the final hand of the 1981 WSOP when Stu Ungar sent his A-Q to do battle against Perry Green for all the marbles.

## ACTION HAND 18

### Playing A-Q Heads-Up at the WSOP

In the last hand of the 1981 WSOP championship event, tournament expert Perry Green and the legendary Stu Ungar went to the center with drawing hands to duke it out for the gold bracelet and the prize money.

With the blinds at $4,000/$8,000, Green held the 10♣ 9♦ on the button and made a modest raise to $16,000. Ungar looked down at the A♥ Q♥ and reraised $25,000 more. Green made a very marginal call. The flop came 8-7-4.

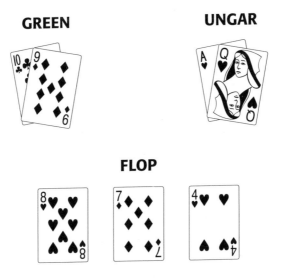

**GREEN**

**UNGAR**

**FLOP**

Both men flopped a big draw. Ungar had the nut flush draw with two overcards to the flop. Green had an open-ended straight draw and two overcards. The way the betting went was rather interesting in that both Ungar and Green acted quickly on the flop. Without hesitation, Ungar went for the kill—he bet $100,000.

Immediately, Green called with his last $78,000 in chips. The pot had well over $200,000 in it, which was close to one-third of the total chips in play. If Green had won the pot, it would have put him into a more competitive position, although he still would not have the lead. The turn card was the 4♣, which paired the board but didn't help either one of them. The Q♦ came on the river, pairing Ungar's hand, although it didn't matter because he would've won anyway with ace-high.

## GREEN            UNGAR

## THE FINAL BOARD

Ungar and Green actually played three key hands against each other during the tournament, and Stuey won all of them. Ungar won with K-K against Green's A-Q when an ace flopped and a king came on the turn. Ungar also won with A♣ J♣ against Green's 10♣ 2♣, and he won the final hand. However, Green was incredibly lucky against the other players. Green would have been eliminated earlier on, but he hit a two-outer to make a bigger set against Bobby Baldwin's set. If Baldwin had won the pot, he would have become the chip leader. Thus, the entire course of the tournament was affected. Ungar was lucky to win his hands against Green, and Green was lucky to beat some of the other players to get to the final table.

Skill and luck are a powerful combination.

# HOW TO PLAY A-J AND A-10

If A-Q is a trouble hand, imagine how dangerous A-J and A-10 are! These are hands that can take no heat whatsoever before the flop at practically any stage of the tournament.

A-J is a little bit stronger than A-10 because of its higher kicker, but A-10 gains some value from the 10—although it's a weak kicker, it can make a straight. As usual, being suited is strictly a bonus. Occasionally you will have to take a stand with these types of hands when, for example, your stack has deteriorated or another player is so short-stacked that he has to play cards that he usually wouldn't.

Generally speaking, these are limping hands from middle to late position when others have entered the pot, and you sometimes can raise with them from late position when no one has entered. But discard them if anyone plays back at you.

# HOW TO PLAY K-Q

In no-limit hold'em, K-Q is a trap hand. Unless you flop something like J-10-9, A-J-10, two kings and a queen, or even two pair, you're in dire circumstances with this hand. You especially wouldn't want to play king-queen in a full ring game, and the same can be said for Q-J. In fact, I give a little more value to J-10 because you can make more straights with the hand than you can make with either K-Q or Q-J.

| KEY CONCEPT |
| --- |
| K-Q is a trap hand in no-limit hold'em. |

## ACTION HAND 19

### Playing K-Q in Late Position

Suppose you're playing in a $2,000 tournament and are dealt the K♣ Q♦. Everybody passes to you on the button. How do you play the hand?

I might raise to try to knock out the two blinds, but that is the only place that I would raise with the hand. Otherwise, I treat K-Q the same as 3-2, like it's the plague. Although it helps if the K-Q is suited, that still doesn't change the fact that this combination can get you into big trouble.

Now suppose you are on the button with K-Q and a player raises in front of you. What do you do? I surely would not stand a raise with this hand, or raise with it myself. But let's say that you decide to gamble and raise with the K♠ Q♥ from a middle position. One opponent calls your raise. The flop comes:

### YOUR HAND

### FLOP

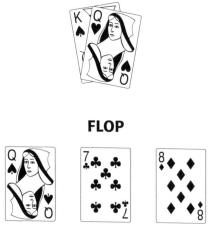

Now what are you going to do? You have top pair with second kicker. In other words, you don't have anything in a *raised* pot! If your opponent called your raise with an A-Q, he has you beaten already. He also might have called with A-A, K-K, Q-Q, 7-7, 8-8, or 8-7 suited. People do call raises with those types of hands, you know.

See the kind of trap you can get yourself into with K-Q?

## Playing K-Q in the Blinds

You are in the little blind with the K♥ Q♦. Everybody has passed to you. What do you do?

In this case, you can raise the big blind, even though you are out of position and will have to act first after the flop. Some players will call a small raise from the big blind with hands that aren't very good because they already have money in the pot, but the chances are good that you'll win the pot right there with your preflop raise.

Another type of connecting hand is an ace with a wheel card. It's a tricky hand to play because your kicker is so weak. The next chapter discusses optimal tournament strategy when you've dealt an ace with a baby card.

# WINNING WITH ACE/WHEEL CARD

In order to play an ace with a wheel card profitably, the right set of circumstances should be in place. Ace-baby suited (or unsuited) is not a hand that you should play from an early position. The hand is of little value to you from up front because if an ace comes on the flop and you bet it, you have no kicker if somebody decides to play with you. Obviously the best flop for ace-small suited is three to your suit or three wheel cards, but the odds against a flop like that are so great that you will definitely lose a lot of money in the long run if you play ace-wheel card every time it is dealt to you.

## PLAYING ACE/BABY IN LATE POSITION

Suppose you are in middle to late position and a couple of players have limped in. Since it's developing into a multiway pot, you might limp with ace-small and see the flop cheaply. But you don't raise with it, you limp. If you get a good flop in multiway action you have the chance to win a nice pot.

You don't want to stand a raise with A-4, and you don't want to play it heads-up. So, when you call a limp bet, be prepared to throw it away if someone raises behind you. Folding against a raise should be a part of your thinking even before you limp into the pot.

Suppose you're in the cutoff seat or on the button and no one has entered the pot. Should you raise with ace-small? No, you don't want to put yourself in a situation where you can't get rid of this type of hand before the flop.

Personally, I never play this hand aggressively. (In no-limit circles we call it a sucker hand.) Let's say that you raise on the button and the small blind calls the raise. He probably has an ace or a pocket pair, and almost any kicker that he has with his ace will be higher than your wheel card. If his kicker also is a wheel card, more often than not you're still not the favorite if an ace falls on the board.

As I have maintained for years, if four or five players in front of you don't have a hand, there's a good chance that one or two of the players behind you do. That is why you limp rather than raise with ace-small in late position—you cannot stand a reraise, you have to release the hand. If you raise and get called, you don't have a hand; and if you want to go further with it, you have to be prepared to bluff unless you catch a flop. Why put yourself in that kind of situation? Your goal is to always be in control.

> **KEY CONCEPT**
>
> If four or five players in front of you don't have a hand, there's a good chance that one or two players behind you do have one.

## PLAYING BLIND AGAINST BLIND

When you're in the small blind against the big blind only, you have three options: raise, fold, or call. If you just call, you might get yourself into trouble; if you fold, you stay out of trouble; raise, and you might win the pot right there. If you have observed that your opponent usually defends his blind, forget about raising. Instead, consider limping against him. If he is someone who raises all the time, he might raise just because you limped. Depending on the type of player he is, you can reraise him; against a different sort, fold if he raises. What you decide to do depends on the kind of read you put on your opponent.

What about playing hands like A-6, A-7, or A-8? None of these ace-middle-card hands can make a straight—your best result is the nut flush if the hand is suited, or two pair if you hit your kicker. You're just throwing your money away if you play them. However, keep in mind that in heads-up action, any ace is far stronger than at a full table.

## *ACTION HAND 20*

### Playing Ace/Baby at the Hall of Fame

At the final table of the 2002 Hall of Fame championship tournament, Howard Lederer faced Peter Costa in heads-up no-limit action with Costa ahead in the chip count. Lederer held the A♦ 4♦. Costa had K♣ 6♥. The flop came:

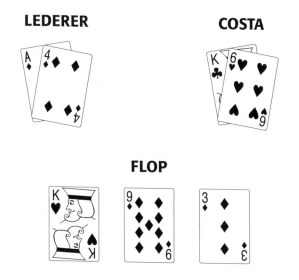

**LEDERER**

**COSTA**

**FLOP**

Lederer flopped the nut flush draw with an overcard to the flop. Costa flopped top pair with a lousy kicker. He bet $30,000 and Lederer, seeing a chance to catch up and grab the victory, raised all-in.

"I can't find a reason to lay the hand down," Costa said, and called the raise. The turn and river brought Lederer no help, and Costa won the title.

## ACTION HAND 21

### Playing Ace/Baby at the Queens Classic

At the Four Queens Classic in 1996, Doyle Brunson and I were playing heads-up for the title in the $5,000 no-limit hold'em event. Holding the A♠ 2♠, I raised a significant amount before the flop. Doyle called with J♦ 9♣. The flop came A♥ J♠ 9♠.

Doyle came out betting with his two pair. I flopped top pair with a lousy kicker, and had the nut flush draw to go along with it. I liked my chances, so I moved all-in. With more chips than I had, Doyle apparently liked his chances too. He called.

At the end of the hand, the board looked like this:

| T.J. | DOYLE |
|------|-------|
|  |  |

### THE FINAL BOARD

"Hell, aren't there any more spades in this deck?" I asked the dealer. Doyle won the pot and the championship.

This hand demonstrates the role that luck plays in poker. You might make the right raise with the best hand, but that doesn't guarantee you're going to like the result. However, one

WSOP champion loved the results he got with ace-baby at the final table, as you will find out in the next action hand.

## ACTION HAND 22

### Playing Ace/Wheel Card at the WSOP

In the last hand at the final table of the 2008 WSOP championship tournament, Peter Eastgate had a commanding chip lead over Ivan Demidov. Eastgate limped into the pot with A-5 offsuit and Demidov checked behind him with a suited 4-2. The board looked like this at the end of the deal:

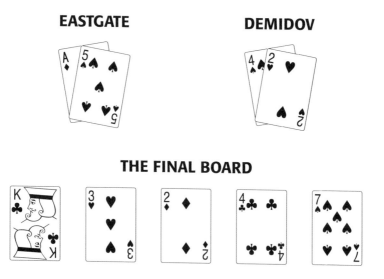

**EASTGATE**          **DEMIDOV**

**THE FINAL BOARD**

Demidov had the lead on the flop with a pair of deuces, and Eastgate had an inside straight draw to a wheel. He led at the pot and Demidov called. When the 4♣ showed up on the turn, Demidov must've thought that he had the winning hand with two pair, not knowing that Eastgate had him dominated with a wheel. He checked in an apparent attempt to check-raise Demidov and take the pot. Eastgate bet $2 million and Demidov came over the top with a raise to $6 million. But rather than laying down his hand as Demidov had hoped, Eastgate called.

When the 7♠ fell on the river, Demidov made his move, going all-in for the rest of his chips. Eastgate called with the winning hand to become the youngest world champion in history at age 22—until Joe Cada topped his record by winning it the next year at age 21.

# WINNING WITH MIDDLE PAIRS & CONNECTORS

Pocket tens and jacks (closely followed by queens) are two of the most difficult hands to play in no-limit hold'em. Although it's better to have J-J than 10-10, one advantage of getting dealt 10-10 is that you are somewhat more likely to make a straight with a 10, making it is less likely that an opponent will make one since you hold two of the four tens in your hand.

## HOW TO PLAY POCKET TENS

There are times in tournaments when you might play 10-10 like you would play 2-2, especially in the early stages of a big buy-in tournament when lots of chips are in play and the blinds are small. You don't put a lot of heat on the pot yourself and you don't take any heat to the hand. You might just slip in and hope to flop a set, not getting too involved if you don't.

If nobody in front of you has entered the pot, you can bring it in for a raise with 10-10—but if you get reraised, throw your tens away without any hesitation. Suppose someone has limped in first position and you're sitting in second position. In this case, you should be very reluctant to raise. Why? Because if a player calls your raise and then another opponent sitting in a later position reraises, you probably don't have the best hand. However, if someone limps in from early position and you're sitting in the last two seats, you definitely can raise with 10-10. If the limper comes back over the top, you can fold.

Be very cautious on the flop if you don't flop a set. Remember that there are four bigger cards that can beat your tens, so if an overcard hits the flop, you can't play your hand confidently. When you have pocket tens, it's likely that one or more overcards will come on the flop, whereas with jacks it's about even money.

## When You're in Early to Middle Position

When you're sitting in early to middle position with pocket tens, you have two options. You can bring it in for a raise, especially if you're the first one in the pot. Just decide in advance that you aren't going to take any serious heat with the hand. If someone raises behind you, it's usually time to bail out.

You also can limp with pocket tens, whether you are the first one in or one or two limpers are already in the pot. If you get any heat before the flop it's usually a pass. For example, in the early stages of a big buy-in tournament when lots of chips are in play, just calling a minimum bet certainly is a viable strategy. On the flop, you want to hit a set—and if you don't, you can get away from them without losing much money because you only limped before the flop.

## When You're in Late Position

Suppose you are in late position. Five or six opponents have passed and either one or no limpers have entered the pot. In this scenario, you should bring it in for a raise with pocket tens.

## *ACTION HAND 23*

### Playing 10-10 in Late Position

Suppose you have pocket tens in the cutoff seat. You're the first one in the pot, so you bring it in for a raise. The big blind calls. The board comes:

## YOUR HAND

## FLOP

The big blind checks to you, and you bet. Then he comes over the top with a reraise. What do you do?

You can't possibly like your hand when someone comes over the top of you—either he thinks you're on a steal, or he has a big hand and is trying to suck you in. If you have only a relatively small amount of chips left, you might go with the hand, but if you have a lot of chips, pass or use your own judgment on the hand. There are situations when your opponent might raise with 9-9, 8-8 or even A-7. Your knowledge of his play should guide your decision to continue or simply fold and get two new cards on the next deal.

In other words, be very cautious when you flop an overpair to the board. You can bet, of course, but if an opponent comes over the top, you can be in a world of trouble. Players like to trap in this type of situation.

## Playing 10-10 in the Late Stage

In the later stages of the tournament you might have to take a stand with your tens because of your chip position. Also, as the table gets shorter (the number of players is reduced), there is the tendency for more rags to be dealt. Therefore, tens improve in value in short-handed play. But don't let yourself get lulled to sleep during this stage. A lot of people excuse their faulty play by saying, "Well, I knew he didn't have much of a hand." Remember that it's always possible for someone to have a big hand—I've seen three-handed tables at which pocket aces, kings and queens were dealt!

You must be prepared to play differently against different opponents in different scenarios. If you aren't willing to tailor your play to the situation, you can get broke to 10-10 (or any other hand) very easily. So even though tens increase in value at a short-handed table, keep all of these other factors in mind when you play them.

# HOW TO PLAY 9-9, 8-8 AND 7-7

Middle pairs should be played very cautiously. You can raise with them from late position if you are the first one in the pot, but be prepared to pitch them if you get played with. If you get called, play them carefully after the flop.

Your chip position often dictates how to play middle pairs. There are times when you are forced to play them—for example, when you're very low on chips and believe that you probably won't get a better hand to play. That's when you take a stand with middle pairs.

Of course, the bigger the pair the better off you are, and the smaller the pair the more vulnerable you are, but for all practical purposes there isn't a lot of difference in the way that you play these middle pairs. Although 9-9 is a little stronger hand than 7-7 or 8-8, and can be played in more or less the same way as 10-10, the biggest difference is that 9-9, 8-8 or

7-7 don't give you as good a chance to make a straight, unless a 10 or 5 hits the board. You can't stand much heat with these hands, and you don't want to put much heat on the pot with them either. When you're playing heads-up for the money and the bracelet, however, a middle pocket pair can look like pocket aces to you. Pocket nines won the world championship for a brash 24-year-old back in 1989.

## ACTION HAND 24

### Playing 9-9 at the WSOP

When Phil Hellmuth faced off against Johnny Chan at the final table of the 1989 WSOP championship event, he was just 24 years old. Chan had won the world championship in 1987 and 1988, and was in position to win his third title in a row.

With the blinds at $5,000/$10,000 with a $2,000 ante, Hellmuth looked down at the 9♠ 9♣ in the small blind. He opened the betting for $35,000. Chan had a decent hand for heads-up play, the A♠ 7♠, and raised $130,000. Without hesitation, Hellmuth shoved $1 million into the middle. Chan puzzled about what to do for quite a while, finally calling all-in with his remaining $450,000 in chips. The flop came K♣ 10♥ K♦.

The flop didn't look that bad for Chan: All he needed to win the pot was an ace or a 10 to give him two higher pair than Hellmuth's kings and nines. He picked some extra outs on when the Q♠ hit the turn—an ace, 10, jack or queen would give him the victory. But it was not to be. The final board looked like this:

## HELLMUTH

## CHAN

## THE FINAL BOARD

The 6♠ on the river wiped out Chan's chance to go down in history for winning three titles in a row. Hellmuth won the title, his first gold bracelet, and the distinction of being the youngest player ever to win the championship, a record that held for 19 years until Peter Eastgate won it at age 22 in 2008. Eastgate also won a lot more money than Hellmuth: First place paid $9,152,416 in 2008 compared to $755,000 in 1989. Eastgate's reign as youngest-ever World Champion of Poker was short-lived—Joe Cada snatched that title from the young Dane just one year later. And strangely, with the same hand that Hellmuth had played 20 years earlier.

In the final hand of the Main Event at the 2009 WSOP, Joe Cada held the 9♦ 9♣ to Darvin Moon's Q♦ J♦. Cada made his standard raise of $3 million preflop only to see Moon reraise to $8 million. Leading Moon in the chip count, Cada shoved his huge chip stack to the middle. Put to the test, Moon paused briefly before deciding to call the young pro's all-in bid for the title. The 46-year-old logger and the 21-year-old pro turned over their cards and started sweating the flop with $8,547,042 hanging in the balance.

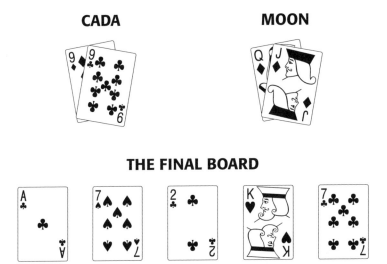

**CADA**

**MOON**

**THE FINAL BOARD**

Thus Cada took youngest-winner honors at the WSOP only one year after Eastgate had dethroned Hellmuth after his 19-year reign. Of course, by the time these young men won their first WSOP title, Hellmuth already had 11 titles to his credit.

# HOW TO PLAY MIDDLE SUITED CONNECTORS

Middle connectors are hands that you play in side games to try to take somebody off. In tournaments, one big drawback is always staring you in the face—you can't go back to your pocket when you lose all your chips.

You want to play small pots with middle suited connectors and stay away from big pots. You shouldn't lead with drawing hands on the flop unless you're prepared to stand a raise—for example, when you have a straight draw, a flush draw, and two overcards to the board. You can lead if you flop a straight, two pair, or a set. Play it strong if a good card comes your way on fourth street, but don't get involved early. Give yourself a chance to get away from the hand if you don't get any help.

## When You're in Early Position

The 9-8 suited is interesting in that it has a lot of potential to be a takeoff hand in the right situations, but be warned—it is a chip burner if you don't play it properly.

Playing this hand is an absolute no-no in early position because it can't stand any pressure. Always remember that the chips you do not lose on bad hands will be available to you later to possibly double or triple up with on your good hands. It's hell to lose a lot of chips on lousy hands, finally wake up with a hand, double up with it, and then find yourself right back where you started, rather than being ahead. You have to think about all these things in tournament play—and especially when you're thinking about playing hands such as 10-9, 9-8, 8-7, or 7-6 suited from up front.

Any time you flop nothing more than an open-ended straight draw with your middle connectors, you cannot bet. If you have other outs in addition to the straight draw, you might call a bet. Just remember that if you get played with, somebody probably has a draw-out hand.

## When You're in Late Position

When two or more limpers have entered the pot, you might occasionally play middle connectors from the cutoff seat or the button. If everyone passes to you on the button and you have the 10♥ 9♥, you have to fold. This advice might be contrary to the way you've seen people play on television. I realize that some players like to limp with middle connectors in this situation, but what are you trying to accomplish when you do that? If nobody has called in front of you and you limp from the cutoff seat or the button, where is the value in the hand? If either the button or the small blind calls, you could be a big underdog. And if only the big blind plays, even if he only holds a hand as weak as J-6 offsuit, he's still a favorite over you.

Remember that if nobody in front of you has a hand, somebody behind you might. McEvoy calls it the "bunching factor," meaning that if no one has big cards up front, it is somewhat more likely that big cards are bunched around back. This concept is especially important to remember when you're in late position with only the blinds yet to act. If a lot of players have passed, it's likely that none of them are holding big cards. It then becomes more likely that one of the blind hands does have big cards—and one of them may wake up with a premium hand in these situations.

---

### KEY CONCEPT

If no one has big cards up front, it is somewhat more likely that big cards are bunched around back.

---

The only time that I see value in middle-connector hands such as 10♥ 9♥ or 9♣ 8♣ in no-limit tournament play is when you hold them in the big blind in an unraised pot, or when you can call for half a bet from the small blind. (Even then, I would fold if the big blind raises.) If the flop comes 9 high, you're not going to play aggressively. Remember that a lot of people like to play ace-anything—A-9, A-10, A-8—for the minimum bet.

Of course, there are exceptions to this general advice. We've reviewed Cada's winning hand at the 2009 WSOP, but it was a key hand that he played earlier against Moon that put him in position to win the title.

## *ACTION HAND 25*

### Playing Middle Connectors at the WSOP

In heads-up action at the final table of the 2009 WSOP, Moon was ahead in the chip count when he and Cada played a key hand that affected the outcome of the match. Holding the J♥ 9♦ on the button, Cada made his standard raise of $3 million to see the flop. Moon called with the 8♠ 7♠. Here came the flop: 10♣ 9♥ 5♦.

With a straight draw, Moon checked. Cada checked behind him with middle pair. The dealer turned over the 10♦ on fourth street. When Moon checked, Cada fired another $3 million at the pot. With only an open-ended straight draw and no diamonds for a flush draw, Moon went all-in, apparently trying to represent trip tens. Cada went into the think tank. When he called all-in, the crowd jumped to its feet. If Cada lost this hand, he would lose the tournament. Tournament director Jack Effel asked Moon and Cada to turn their hands face up. After the dealer dealt the river card, the final board looked like this:

### CADA

### MOON

## THE FINAL BOARD

Cada doubled through Moon on this hand with two pair, tens and nines, and extended his lead a few hands later when he played 10♣ 9♣ to make two pair on the K♠ 10♦ 7♥ 8♥ 9♦ and siphon more chips from Moon's dwindling stack.

When you're playing heads-up for the whole enchilada, the strength of your hand isn't always what counts the most—it's your chips, position, feel ... and heart.

---

**KEY CONCEPT**

Just because any two cards can win in poker doesn't mean that you should play them—unless everything else is perfect!

---

# WINNING WITH SMALL PAIRS

Suppose you've made it to the final table in a no-limit hold'em tournament. The table is six-handed and you look down at 6-6 on the button. The action is passed to you. Time and time again I've seen players sitting around back with a small pair move in their whole stack if everybody passes to them. I think it's a horrible play, yet I've seen players do it—and wind up losing their entire stack because their small pair didn't hold up when one of the blinds called their all-in raise. Let me ask you this: When you've worked that hard to get to the final table, why would you risk losing everything to such a crappy hand? Once again, remember that if several players in front of you don't have anything, there's a decent chance that one of the players behind you *will*.

In this situation, it might be okay to make a small or even decent-sized raise. For example, say that the antes are $200 and the blinds are $400/$800 at a six-handed table. There is $2,400 in the pot, and you have $15,000 in front of you. If you want to raise, why not bring it in for $3,000? That's plenty—if you get reraised or outflopped, you can get away from the hand without losing all your chips to it. But what are you going to do if you move in your whole stack and get called?

While there are certain situations when you can play small pocket pairs, you usually should avoid playing them. If you stand a little raise in no-limit with a baby pair, it's almost always because you have huge implied odds, a lot more chips than the other players, and you're getting multiway action.

If three or four players have called in front of you in a raised pot and you're sitting around back with a lot of chips, obviously it's nice to have a small pocket pair such as fours. But playing heads-up or even a three-way pot isn't a good idea. From a front position, I throw 4-4 away as though it's 7-2. You can only stand a raise with 4-4 or 5-5 if you're getting very good pot odds, and obviously you're hoping to flop a set and rake in a good pot. But if you don't flop a set to your little pair, there are very few scenarios where you can play them. In other words, you need to get very lucky to win with small pairs. Playing hands like 4-4 heads-up for a raise is almost always a mistake. People who move in with these types of hands are just asking to get broke.

Yet time and time again you see players who are strapped for chips and clinging to life play these hands: One player has $3,000 in chips, looks down at a baby pair, and moves in with everything he's got. If he gets called, he's an 11 to 10 favorite at best, but he could also be a 4.5 to 1 dog. Of course, if you're anteing more than $200 or so, and you have only $800 in chips with the blinds coming up, that's a different situation. In that scenario, you might play the hand, but with $3,000 or $4,000 in chips, you have time to wait for a better hand.

Small pairs are takeoff hands in no-limit *when you have a lot of chips.* Keep in mind that 4-4 is only an 11 to 10 favorite over 6-5. When you take that into account, there are a lot of hands better than two fours. Pocket fives have a little more value because 5 is a straight card.

Players often talk about the fact that A-K is only an 11 to 10 underdog to a pocket pair. But what they don't realize is that if you have 6-6 and your opponent has 8-7, his hand also is only an 11 to 10 dog to your pair of sixes. It isn't just the A-K that is the underdog: *Any* two overcards are an 11 to 10 underdog to a pair. Further, if the overcards are suited, they are slightly smaller dogs to the pocket pair. These numbers are what make moving in your whole stack with a small or medium pair such a bad play.

In short-handed action, small pairs take on more importance. And when you're playing heads-up, they're even more powerful. In 2006, twenty-one years after he won the world championship, Phil Hellmuth found himself in a bind: The poor guy had "only" won nine WSOP events and was trailing Doyle Brunson and Johnny Chan by one title in the hyped-up bracelet race. In the $1,000 buy-in no-limit hold'em event, he was playing his third final table trying to catch up with Doyle and Johnny when the key hand of the tournament came up. Here's how it happened:

## ACTION HAND 26

### A Pair of Fives Adds Up to Ten

Juha Helppi, a fine young player from Finland, had a 3 to 1 chip lead over Phil Hellmuth when this key hand developed heads-up for the bracelet. Before the flop, Juha raised $90,000 with the A♥ 6♦ on the button. Phil answered by pushing all-in with the 5♥ 5♠, and Juha covered the bet. The flop came:

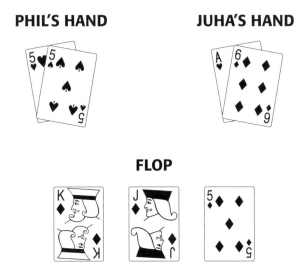

**PHIL'S HAND**          **JUHA'S HAND**

**FLOP**

Juha probably was wishing he had the A♦ instead of the A♥, but still he had flopped a four flush and an overcard to the board. Phil, of course, flopped trip fives. After receiving the signal from the tournament director, the dealer slowly dealt the turn card—the Q♦—giving Juha the flush. The only way he could lose this hand was if the board paired. Guess what? The final board looked like this:

**PHIL'S HAND**          **JUHA'S HAND**

**THE FINAL BOARD**

His full house put Phil put back in the race against Doyle and Johnny. He went on win his tenth bracelet when his A-J held up against Juha's A-9 in the final hand of the match.

It wasn't the first time that a small pocket pair won a title at the WSOP. One of the most famous hands in WSOP history happened at the 1993 final table when the action was three-handed. The pivotal hand was played between A-K and 6-6. The next action hand tells you what happened.

## ACTION HAND 27

### A Low Pair Levels Big Slick in a Classic WSOP Hand

The final table of the Main Event at the 1993 WSOP was down to three-way action between John Bonetti, Jim Bechtel, and Glen Cozen, who was a distant third. I knew that Bechtel liked to play every hand from behind—that is, check with the best hand and try to trap—and I had warned my good friend Bonetti about that.

When the key hand that decided the outcome of the tournament came up, Bechtel had a relatively small lead with $1,150,000 to Bonetti's $935,000. Cozen was in a distant third with $95,000, most of which he had won in an earlier hand with Bonetti when his K-J bested Bonetti's 9-9.

Bechtel raised $30,000 on the button with the 6♦ 6♣ and Bonetti called in the small blind with the A♦ K♣. After thinking for two minutes, Cozen also called the raise, but we don't know what he held because there were no pocket cams at that time. The flop came:

**BONETTI**   **BECHTEL**   **COZEN**

**FLOP**

When Bonetti hit his king on the flop, giving him top pair/top kicker, he checked intending to check-raise Bechtel or Cozen if either of them bet. Cozen also checked, but it looked as though Bechtel took the bait when he shoved $75,000 to the middle. Bonetti quickly raised to $180,000, Cozen just as quickly folded, and Bechtel just called.

Right then, neon lights should've started flashing in Bonetti's head. I understand that when you're in the heat of battle, sometimes you just don't see every possibility, but you have to stay alert. I had told him earlier that Bechtel is weaker leading with a hand than he is calling with one. In other words, if Bechtel had been leading with his hand, Bonetti's A-K probably was good—but Bechtel was just calling, and that made all the difference in the world. Bonetti should've thought, "I've got all these chips and Glen Cozen only has a few. Am I gonna get broke in this pot, or am I gonna check it down and throw it away if Bechtel bets into me?"

Once Bechtel called him—and taking into account his chip position versus Cozen—Bonetti had to shut down. He couldn't lose any more money to the hand because of the payout difference between first, second and third place.

But Bonetti didn't fold.

## TURN

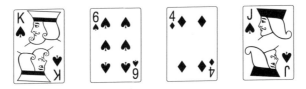

When the J♠ fell on the turn, Bonetti moved all-in. After a short deliberation, Bechtel called. The crowd rose to its feet. Jim Van Patten, tournament announcer, and Jim Albrecht, WSOP manager, surmised that someone either had a set or a flush. Tournament director Jack McClelland gave the signal for Bonetti and Bechtel to turn their cards face up. This was the first time we knew what they held, as pocket cams didn't come into existence until over a decade later.

When Bonetti saw Bechtel's pocket sixes, he threw his A-K in the air, realizing that he had no outs to win the hand on the river. If a king fell, he'd make trips, but Bechtel would make a full house. If another spade came off, Bechtel would make a flush. We don't know what the river card was because the video of the event did not reveal its rank or suit, but obviously it made no difference in the outcome. Bechtel won the hand with trip sixes, sending Bonetti out third and easing Cozen into second. A few hands later, Bechtel became the 1993 World Champion when his J♠ 6♠ beat Cozen's 7♦ 4♥.

In his post-tournament interview, Bonetti told Albrecht, "Those things happen. I'll have to wait for another year." But that year never came for my good friend John.

# WINNING WITH SMALL CONNECTORS AND TRASH HANDS

Playing small connectors seems to have become fashionable these days in no-limit hold'em events. Maybe it's because players are willing to take more risks than previously, or maybe they're confusing the small ball betting strategy with playing small hands. But I still maintain that you're just asking for trouble when you play drawing hands in no-limit tournaments, no matter how big or small your cards are. With these types of connectors, your big decision always comes on the flop.

As I've said before, I try to stay away from as many draws in no-limit hold'em as I possibly can, especially in tournaments. And I am never going to open a pot with them.

The only times that I am willing to play small connectors is when the pot is multiway, or occasionally in a heads-up, big stack against big stack situation.

## THE DANGER OF DRAWING TO SMALL CONNECTORS

What if you flop a draw to this type of hand? In tournaments, draws are death—you're always taking the worst of it because you're always the underdog to a made hand when you call a bet to draw to your hand.

For example, suppose you have the 5♦ 4♠ in a back position. Someone makes a little raise preflop, everybody folds, and you decide to call. The flop comes:

## YOUR HAND

## FLOP

Your opponent bets at the pot. I would never flat call with this drawing hand against a bet. I would either raise him right on the flop to try to blow him out of the pot, or throw away the hand. Why? Because if you don't make the draw on the first card off, he's going to come after you again and then you will have to dump your hand.

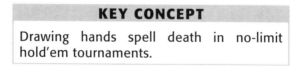

### KEY CONCEPT

Drawing hands spell death in no-limit hold'em tournaments.

Now suppose you hold this same 5-4 and several players are in the pot. An opponent bets at the pot, someone calls, and then it's up to you. What do you do? *Nothing has changed.* If you make a play at the pot by raising and both of your opponents fold, you will win double money, true—but you're also taking the chance of getting called and losing money to the hand. And that is why I either fold or raise rather than call.

If a player bets and another players calls, what do I have with the 5-4 on the 2-3-10 flop? I have eight outs twice if my cards are still in the deck—if neither of them is holding two aces or two sixes. But I am not looking to get pot odds in a no-limit tournament. Anytime you make a play in a tournament and get beaten for all of your chips, you're out of the tournament, no matter what pot odds you had on the flop. This thought always has to be in the back of your mind, but don't let it scare you so much that you freeze up. If you have fear in no-limit hold'em tournament action, you'd better not play the game.

## Calling a Raise with Small Connectors

Let's say that you're playing in the early stage when the blinds are $25/$50. You are in late-middle position preflop with the 7♣ 6♣ and two limpers have come into the pot in front of you. If you don't think that you will be raised, you can call with this hand. But if someone puts in a pot-sized raise, you dump the hand in a New York minute.

When is it correct to call a raise with small connectors? When you are on the button or the cutoff seat with a lot of chips against an opponent with a lot of chips, there is nothing wrong with calling a *small* raise with 7-6 or 5-4 suited, for example. Your opponent will almost never put you on this hand, and if you don't flop to it, you can get rid of it right away. You're simply taking a shot at taking down a big pot or busting somebody with your small suited connectors. This is a situation where "feel" comes into the game.

One of the most famous hands in WSOP Main Event history was played in a situation similar to this. Here's the story of what happened.

## ACTION HAND 28

### Making a Mint with a Minimum Hand

When the final table at the Main Event of the 2003 WSOP started, Chris Moneymaker was the chip leader. One by one, his opponents fell by the wayside until it got down to three-handed action with Chris in the lead against Dan Harrington and Sammy Farha. That's when Chris played a heads-up hand against "Action Dan" that set up the final duel between Chris and Sammy. Dan held the K♦ 6♠ while Chris had 10♠ 9♣. On the 2♦ 6♦ 10♦ flop, Dan flopped second pair and a big flush draw to Chris's top pair with a weak kicker. When Dan bet $150,000, Chris raised enough to put him all-in. On the short stack, Dan called. The final board read 2♦ 6♦ 10♦ A♥ A♠ to send him home in third place.

Chris and Sammy started playing heads-up for all the marbles with Chris in the lead by $5,490,000 in chips to Sammy's $2,900,000. After sparring for about 20 hands, Chris was even further in the lead by $6.6 million to $1.8 million when the final hand came up.

Holding the J♥ 10♦, Sammy raised to $100,000 from the small blind and Chris called with the 5♦ 4♠. The now-famous flop came J♠ 5♠ 4♣.

Moneymaker checked his two pair to Farha, who bet $175,000 with top pair. When Moneymaker answered by raising $300,000, Farha moved in with all his chips. Naturally, Moneymaker called. Here's how the board looked at the end:

**MONEYMAKER**          **FARHA**

## THE FINAL BOARD

And that's how a novice at live tournament poker took down a top pro for a then record payday of $2.5 million and the 2003 World Championship of Poker.

I've heard people say that Moneymaker just got lucky on this hand, that he was on a lucky streak throughout the entire tournament, but let me ask you this: Have you ever heard of a tournament winner who didn't get lucky at some point in the event? Sure, he even said that he got lucky here and there, but he also had enough skill and heart to outplay some of the world's best tournament players. In the final hand, he was correct in calling Farha's opening raise with 5-4—in fact, he could've called with 7-2 and still been right. Checking to Farha on the flop and then following with a relatively small raise when Farha bet was just plain ol' good play.

He had also built his confidence by the time the final table began. In his Poker Pages commentary, Mark Napolitano said, "Chris is very confident and doesn't seem to be fazed by Sammy any more. Maybe he is naïve, but that may be why he isn't feeling the intimidation of the other players. And if they see that this doesn't make him lose concentration, then they don't have any more weapons to go after him other than the luck of the cards."

Luck, skill and heart—that's what it takes to win the big ones.

# WHEN TO PLAY TRASH HANDS

Sometimes a tournament situation dictates literally playing any two cards. In other words, you sometimes will have to take a stand with a trash hand because the alternative is even less appealing. I call this the "7-2 Factor." Let's take a look at a tournament situation in which you don't have a real hand, just two useless cards.

Years ago at the Queens Classic we were playing nine-handed at the final table with the ante at $500 and the blinds $3,000/$6,000. Sitting in the big blind, I had a total of $13,000 in chips before I posted the $6,000 big blind and $500 ante. The next hand was going to cost me $3,500 more.

Looking down at my cards, I had 7-2 offsuit. The hand was passed around to the button, who raised. The little blind threw his hand away, and the action was up to me. I did not hesitate to call for one reason—I knew that if the button had ace-something or king-something, I was only a 2 to 1 dog so long as he wasn't paired. However, considering the size of the pot, the odds against me weren't quite that good, so I called. He had A-J, I paired the deuce, won the pot, and went on to win second place.

> ### KEY CONCEPT
> Never allow your stack to get so low on chips that even if you double up, you still won't have enough chips to play with.

The point of this story is that you can never let yourself get so low in chips that even if you double up you still won't have enough chips to play with. In some tournament situations you have to play any two cards. You sometimes are better off going in with a nothing hand than you would be if you anted off your last chips. There's always the chance that you can win the pot without a fight or outflop your opponent. If I had thrown the hand away, I would have had $6,500 left with $3,500 of it going in for the ante and the small blind in the very next pot.

Now suppose I hadn't caught a playable hand in the big blind—I would have had to quadruple my chips just to get back the money that I had before I went through the two blinds. I was better off making a move before I put myself into that kind of untenable situation.

In situations like the one I faced, your fate is practically sealed anyway—if you call and lose, you won't have enough chips to play in any case, and if you fold, you still won't have many chips. So why not give yourself at least some chance of winning? By calling, you're simply making the best of a bad situation.

This strategy worked out quite well for Doyle Brunson when he won his first gold bracelet back in 1976.

## ACTION HAND 29

### Winning with Trash at the WSOP

Doyle Brunson was playing Jesse Alto heads-up at the final table of the 1976 World Series of Poker when he looked down at what has become a famous piece of trash, a 10-2. Alto brought the pot in for a raise with the A♠ J♥, a strong hand in heads-up action. With a 3 to 1 chip lead, Doyle called the raise. He had just beaten Jesse in a big pot and knew that he was steaming. The flop came A♥ J♠ 10♥.

This was a terrific flop for Jesse—top two pair. All Doyle had was third-best pair against a suited and coordinated flop. Of course, he couldn't see how strong Jesse's hand was on the flop, but he knew that he was capable of betting with anything in this situation. So, when Jesse came out betting, Doyle called.

The deuce on the turn gave Doyle two pair, which probably looked pretty good to him heads-up. This time around, Doyle moved in and Jesse called with the rest of his chips and the best hand. Here's how the final board looked:

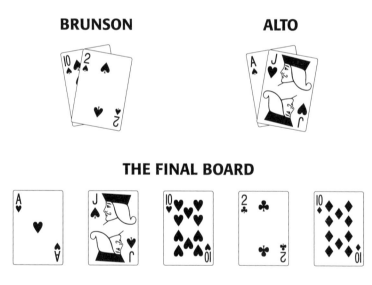

**BRUNSON**

**ALTO**

**THE FINAL BOARD**

Everybody in the audience had to be purely amazed when the 10♦ came on the river to snatch the victory from Jesse and hand it over to Doyle.

You probably know the rest of the story—how Doyle also won the championship the very next year with the same piece of trash, a 10-2, in a heads-up battle with Bones Berland. Unlike his preflop hand in 1976, Doyle had the better hand before the flop in 1977, since Berland only had an 8-5. However, Berland had the better hand on the flop, only to see the tide turn against him when Brunson hit two pair on the turn and filled on the river.

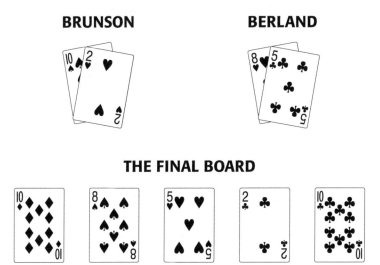

## BRUNSON        BERLAND

## THE FINAL BOARD

Brunson described how the action came down in Dana Smith's book, *The Championship Table*: "I was in the big blind and had 10-2 against Bones Berland. When the flop came out 10-8-5, I checked (my top pair) and he checked (his two pair). The fourth card was a deuce. I bet, he moved in on me, and I called. The last card was another 10, so in both final hands (1976 and 1977), I made a full house with 10-2." Since then, a 10-2 hand has been known as a "Brunson."

## ACTION HAND 30

### A Garbage Hand Cleans Up at the WSOP

On hand 232 of the heads-up match of the 2005 WSOP, Steve Dannenmann raised to $700,000 before the flop with the A♦ 3♣. Joe Hachem called the raise holding a hand usually referred to as garbage, the 7♣ 3♠. Amazingly he flopped a straight!

**HACHEM**          **DANNENMANN**

**FLOP**

Hachem coolly checked to Dannenmann on the flop. With an open-ended straight draw and a three flush, Dannenmann shipped another $700,000 to the middle. Hachem raised $1 million and Dannenmann called to see the turn.

When the A♠ showed up, Hachem bet $2 million. Dannenmann had improved to top pair with an open-ended straight draw, and reraised to $5 million. Hachem announced "All in!" Dannenmann put his tournament future on the line by calling short—if he lost the hand, he'd lose the title. When they turned their hands over to see the river card, Dannenmann realized that he needed to catch a 7 to complete the straight draw, split the pot with Hachem, and stay alive in the biggest event he'd ever played. 'Twas not to be. The final board read:

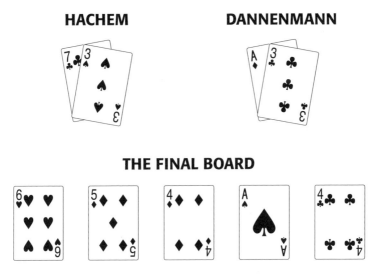

**HACHEM**

**DANNENMANN**

**THE FINAL BOARD**

With the longest final-table battle in WSOP finally over, Hachem was crowned World Champion of Poker to the cheers of his large contingent of fans chanting "Aussie, Aussie, Aussie!" in support of the first Australian to win the Main Event.

This story is a fitting close to our section on no-limit tournament play. Next up is a special chapter with our commentary on key hands that world-class players have played at the Main Event of the World Series of Poker. But first, you'll find some good tips on how to build your stack in McEvoy's following section, "Build Your Stack, Don't Blow It!"

# BUILD YOUR STACK, DON'T BLOW IT!

**TOM MCEVOY**

I played in a major tournament in which the chip leader going into the final table outdistanced his nearest competitor by a 5 to 1 margin—and blew it, finishing in sixth place. You've seen the same kind of thing happen yourself, haven't you? The favorite loses the race to a dark horse when he makes a fatal error or loses a few key hands, or doesn't use common sense in managing his stack.

## YOUR STACK IS YOUR MOST PRECIOUS ASSET IN A TOURNAMENT.

You work hard to build it, like you'd build your dream house. An architect designs a blueprint before he builds, and you must design a tournament game plan to build a competitive war chest. Your building blocks are chips; the more of them you have, the stronger your foundation. In most tournaments, you try to build your stack by about 25 percent during each round in the early and middle stages, and you hope to double up in the later stages. In games like Omaha high-low split, you accumulate chips slowly, whereas in no-limit or pot-limit hold'em, you can double or triple your stack in one hand. The old saying, "It takes money to make money" is true of chips too. A big stack is very intimidating at all stages of a tournament, so that it takes greater strength in your opponents' hands for them to compete against you when you have a tower of chips.

You also need a backup plan for when you suffer big beats. For example, how will you handle things if you get a big hand snapped off, leaving you short-stacked? Your plan should include what to do in other stressful situation (like going all in to call a big raise) and how to play different opponents. You've got to get into your opponents' heads to get some insight into their playing style, which hands they raise with, what kinds of hands they are likely to bluff with, and so on.

> Some players try to win tournaments too early by attempting to accumulate big stacks of chips in the first round or two.

Usually this simply is not going to happen. If you can double up in the first round, you've done a marvelous job, and adding even 50 percent to your stack is an achievement. But it is unrealistic to believe that you can amass three to four times your original stack after only one round of play, unless you catch a tremendous rush of cards.

When you are short-stacked late in the tournament, you frequently will have to take a stand with less than a premium hand. The shorter your stack, the more important it is to use good judgment about when to jeopardize it. This is especially true when you have only one or two bets left, because you know that you will be called by at least the big blind, if not someone with a bigger collection of chips. So you have to wait and then take your best shot. You don't necessarily have to wait for A-K, but you also don't want to risk your chips by going all in with 10-9 or K-7, if you can help it.

# BUILD YOUR STACK, DON'T BLOW IT!

> With a big stack late in the event, you should attack the short stacks at every opportunity.

The more chips you have, the more your options, but even with a massive amount of chips you still have to use good judgment, especially in deciding whether to go up against other big stacks. You have to wait for premium hands before you attack one of the other big boys.

You also can capitalize on the tight play of your opponents by betting more aggressively when they don't have much to play with. Even though they may suspect that you are raising with less than a premium hand, there isn't much that they can do about it if they have an average hand. Big stacks are weapons—use them!

At the final two or three tables, I take a cruise around to see how many short stacks there are, and how many more players need to be eliminated before I can make it to the final table. Sometimes this census affects my playing strategy. For example, if I am on a short stack and I see a couple of other players who have even less, I wait for a prime hand before betting big— especially if the other short stacks are about to get eaten up by the blinds. Of course, I won't throw away aces or kings, because I don't just need enough chips to survive, but enough to go all the way. Never lose sight of the big picture—winning the tournament. But knowing the chip counts of the guys at the other tables, the short stacks in particular, is definitely useful.

> Playing a mid-sized stack is one of the trickiest tournament skills.

In many situations, you will be doing more check-calling with a mid-sized stack. Suppose you entered the pot in late position with K-J and flopped a king, the highest upcard. If there are connecting cards that look dangerous, you could easily run into two pair or a straight draw. Although you may have been leading at the pot, if the river card is a connector that could make two pair or a straight for someone else, you should check-call if it looks like you still have the best hand. Even if you may bet the pot in a side game, it's better to play more conservatively in a tournament, and check-calling is usually the way to go. It also may induce a bluff on the end from a player whose hand did not materialize.

Always be aware of your stack status and what round of the tournament you are in. In the early to middle rounds, chips begin to get redistributed and you need to know who has the taller stacks and who has the shorter ones, and where your stack stands in relation to theirs.

Unfortunately, it's not as easy to build a stack as it is to blow it. You can be sure that the players you're going to read about in the next section knew how to build their stacks to get to the money table—even if a few of them blew their chips after they got there or suffered bad beats on good hands that robbed them of victory. In either case, their stories are instructional and interesting if for no other reason than that they got there.

PART TWO

# KEY HANDS AT THE WORLD SERIES OF POKER
## THE ACTION • THE OUTCOME • THE LESSONS

Key hands turn the tide of fortune—they are the hands of destiny. If you win them, you're in good shape. If you lose them, you're on the rail. Few spectators realize that the key hand in a tournament might be one that was played long before the final table.

For example, the key hand at the 1984 World Series of Poker championship event was not the last hand played between champion Jack Keller and runner-up Cowboy Wolford. In fact, Keller wasn't even involved in the key hand that led him to victory: It was played between Wolford and Jesse Alto, who finished third. And when Jack Straus defeated Dewey Tomko in 1982, it actually was a previous hand that Straus had played and lost, leaving him with only one chip, that led him to eventual victory.

Spectators are often amazed that the winning hand at the final table is so weak. But seasoned tournament veterans understand that in heads-up play, it doesn't take a strong hand to win a showdown, it only takes the best hand, as Doyle Brunson wrote years ago. Brunson is proof positive of this axiom—he won the championship two years in a row with 10-2.

In the years before pocket cams, you didn't know what the players held unless there was a showdown. Viewing poker tournaments was comparable to watching paint dry. Thankfully, many of the early WSOP Main Event final tables were videotaped, so we got to see the players' hole cards at the showdown. For most of the key hands we describe, we watched those vintage tapes or were in the audience. For some, we had to rely on written reports, and for several others we sought the expertise of Dana Smith, author of *The Championship Table*. And a precious few, we wrote from personal experience. T.J. has been there four times and I have been there once.

# KEY HANDS AT THE WSOP FINAL TABLE

## 7-HANDED

From 1981 through 2000, the final table was considered to be only the last six players. Since they usually were the only ones videotaped or televised, finishing seventh was always a huge disappointment. From 1970 through 1977, it was winner-take-all at the WSOP. In 1978-1980, only the top five finalists got a payday. The tradition of paying the top nine began in 1981, the year that Stu Ungar won his second consecutive championship. We begin this chapter with some little-known action from that final table.

## ACTION HAND 31

### Set Over Set Turns the Tide
**Tom McEvoy, Commentary**

For the third time in four years, Bobby Baldwin made it to the final table in 1981 where once again, set over set played a major role in his outcome in the tournament. Two years earlier in eight-handed action at the final table of the 1979 WSOP championship event, Sam Moon had raised with A-A before the flop. Two players called in front of Baldwin, who also called with 8-8. He had won the championship the previous year and was hoping to make it two in a row.

When the flop came 8-6-3, Moon bet $30,000 and Baldwin moved all-in for $45,000 with top set. Moon called, bringing the pot to over $100,000—whoever won it would become the chip leader. On fourth street, Moon spiked an ace and sent Baldwin home in eighth place with no payday, since only five places were paid that year. As Bobby found out, it's tough for a champion to repeat, like Doyle Brunson had done in 1976-77—and like Stu Ungar was about to do.

Now Baldwin was playing at his third final table when, with seven players left, he played a key hand against Perry Green that put Green in position to eventually go to battle heads-up against Stu Ungar for the title. Here's how it happened.

Baldwin was dealt 9-9 and Green was dealt Q-Q. The flop came 9-high: 9♠ 4♥ 3♣.

Baldwin checked his top set to Green, figuring to check-raise him. Green took the bait and bet $40,000. Baldwin then raised $86,000, enough to put Green all-in if he called. Green agonized over it before finally calling with his overpair. When the hands were turned up, Green realized that he was reduced to two outs. A very strong player, Baldwin still had chips left and if he won the hand, he would become the chip leader at the final table. But again, it was not to be.

Here's how the board looked on the river:

### BALDWIN            GREEN

## THE FINAL BOARD

When he hit the two-outer on the river to defeat Baldwin's set of nines, Green went nuts, jumping up and down in celebration. Now very low on chips, Baldwin just sat there with a weak smile on his face realizing that the hand had put Green in position to win the tournament.

The highs and the lows in tournament poker are second to none. When Green realized he was up against Baldwin's trip nines, he probably thought, "Oh, God, I've played all this time and now I'm through." But when the Q♠ hit, his emotions took a u-turn. Suddenly everybody was congratulating him. The ebbs and flows in poker can raise your spirits from the pits to the pinnacle—and unfortunately, vice versa.

## ACTION HAND 32

### Deja Vu With Pocket Kings
**T.J. Cloutier, Commentary**

On the third day of play at the 1992 WSOP, a situation came up seven-handed that is still being discussed in poker circles. Because only six players were filmed at the final table, seventh-place finisher Johnny Chan, who won back-to-back bracelets in 1987-88 and finished second in 1989, did not appear for the TV cameras.

This hand came up between Mike Alsaadi and Hamid Dastmalchi, the chip leader. Hamid raised before the flop with two kings and Mike moved in on him. Mike had made it clear that he was determined to play on the final day when the top six finalists would be televised, and while Hamid was considering whether to call, he announced that he had two aces.

If Hamid calls and loses, he will be second in chips, but still have fairly good chip position. If he calls and wins, he will amass an overwhelming chip lead. If he folds, he will retain his chip lead. He thinks about it, gently taps the table, turns over two kings, and throws them in the muck. True to his word, Mike flashes two aces.

Apparently, Mike didn't want to take the chance of getting drawn out on. I would've taken a different perspective on how to play it, but he was determined not to get his aces cracked so that he could make it to the final day—which he did—although Hamid won the title.

Holding two kings against two aces was not the only time that a tournament leader has made that kind of fold and then gone on to win the tournament. Seven years later at the 1999 Tournament of Champions in Las Vegas, a similar situation came up. David Chiu, the eventual winner, raised on the button with pocket kings when the action was still six or seven-handed. Louis Asmo, a distant second in chips at that time, moved in with two aces from the small blind. Chiu would be the overwhelming leader if he called and won the pot. If he folded, he still will have a pretty good chip lead. Chiu thought things over at length before finally mucking the two kings.

Asmo showed his two aces to the audience. Eventually he came second to Chiu for the title. In these two scenarios, both Dastmalchi and Chiu protected their chip lead by folding pocket kings before the flop and went on to win the tournament. Laydowns like these take balls of iron to make, but champions are steeled to do whatever it takes to win. Think about that if you ever find yourself in a similar situation.

## ACTION HAND 33

### Pocket Rockets Bite the Dust

**T.J. Cloutier, Commentary**

The final table I played at the 1998 WSOP championship event wasn't nearly as exciting as the one that I played in 1988 when I finished fifth to Johnny Chan and Erik Seidel, but anytime you can get to the final table at the WSOP, it's all good. We started the televised action with only five players instead of the usual six because of an unusual situation that came up when we were seven-handed.

I strongly felt that Ben Roberts deserved to be at the televised table with us because he's such a fine player. But a bad thing happened to him along the way. Jan Lundberg moved all-in with 10-10 and Scotty Nguyen called on the button with the A♦ Q♦. Ben moved in from the small blind for all his chips with the best hand in poker, A-A. Everybody in the world knew that Ben had pocket aces, but Scotty called him fast with his suited ace, making it a three-way pot with both Roberts and Lundberg all-in.

The flop came with three diamonds and Scotty knocked Roberts and Lundberg out at the same time. That's why we started with only five players at the televised table, the only time that has ever happened in WSOP history. But if Scotty had lost this hand, he would have been injured and Ben would have had a substantial stack to make a run at the roses.

Before the final table began, Scotty also held A-Q, this time against Jack Keller's Q-Q. Here's how the hand came down: Scotty raised and Jack moved all-in for about $70,000 in chips. Most players would have laid down A-Q against Jack's raise, but not Scotty. He almost beat Jack into the pot, caught an ace, and won the hand.

Scotty played A-Q four times, won with it four times, and wound up winning the world championship—and I can't win with the damned hand! Of course, he got very lucky and that is important in tournament play. So often, it is *when* you make these types of plays that counts—timing is everything. Ace-queen was Scotty's ticket to the top in 1998, but it was a terror for me in 2000 when I played it for the bracelet and the big bucks against Chris Ferguson's A-9.

## ACTION HAND 34

### Pocket Sixes Best Pocket Sevens

T.J. Cloutier, Commentary

A key hand happened before the six-handed televised table at the 2000 WSOP that put Chris Ferguson in a position to really do damage later in the round when he had aces against kings. This is the way the first key hand came up when we were 7-handed: Everyone folded to Jeff Shulman on the button and he brought it in for a raise with 7-7. The small blind folded. Ferguson then came over the top from the big blind for all his chips with 6-6. Shulman called the raise.

Shulman was playing super, but he was inexperienced at that time. He had $1,500,000 in chips and did not need to play any huge pots. In that situation, you are either an 11 to 10 favorite or a 4.5 to 1 dog. You don't figure that you're a 4.5-to-1 favorite when you're holding two sevens in that spot because Ferguson had reraised. Therefore, if Ferguson had two overcards, even if they were only 9-8, Shulman was only an 11 to 10 favorite.

I don't think Shulman was wrong in raising the pot a little bit—he had plenty of chips—but when Ferguson reraised, I believe he should have released the hand. He didn't need to gamble, and he wouldn't have gotten hurt much by losing the chips that he had raised.

So, what happened? Ferguson made trip sixes on the flop and doubled through Shulman, thus putting himself in position to win the whole ballgame.

## ACTION HAND 35

### Aces Beat Kings and Jacks

**T.J. Cloutier, Commentary**

The next key hand happened after Chris Ferguson had won with 6-6 against Jeff Shulman's 7-7. Chris brought it in for a little raise under the gun and I reraised with J-J, making it $200,000 to go. Jeff moved in for all his chips with K-K. Chris called. I knew that my hand was a loser so I released it, leaving me with the $200,000 that I took to the televised table with me.

When Jeff reraised and Chris called, there was only one hand in the world that Chris could've been holding—A-A. It sounds incredible, but three big hands were dealt in seven-handed play. And the best hand won. Chris's aces beat Jeff's kings and in the process, sent Jeff to the rail in seventh place, setting up the final table.

Although Jeff had amassed twice as many chips as anybody else at the table, these two hands took him out of the action. But that's all it takes to lose a tournament. At that time, Jeff didn't have much experience in tournament play, but he has improved his game significantly since then. He made his second appearance at the WSOP championship table in 2009 as part of the now famous November Nine, finishing fifth to eventual winner Joe Cada.

# KEY HANDS AT THE WSOP FINAL TABLE
## 6-HANDED & 5-HANDED

During the 20 years when only the top six final players were videotaped or televised at the WSOP championship table, players felt both jubilant and relieved when they made it to the final table. Some had barely escaped finishing seventh and out of the limelight, while others had hit it big time with the chip lead. Our first hand in this chapter gives you insight into what can happen when you start the final table with plenty of chips.

## ACTION HAND 36

### A Rare Straight Flush at the Final Table
Tom McEvoy, Commentary

Going to the final six at the 1994 WSOP, Vince Burgio was a solid second in the chip count, well ahead of everyone except chip leader Hugh Vincent, who had almost three times as many chips as Burgio. In this key hand, Burgio opened for $30,000 on the button and Russ Hamilton called with the K♣ J♣ from the blind. The flop came 6♣ 7♣ 10♣.

Hamilton led at the pot for $15,000 with his king-high flush. It wasn't a very big bet—it was a suck-in bet, actually. Burgio called. The turn card was the 9♣, which put four cards to the straight flush on board. Hamilton appeared to be in jeopardy—he could be up against the ace-high flush or the nut straight flush. He checked. Burgio checked behind him. Here's how the board looked on the river:

**HAMILTON**       **BURGIO**

## THE FINAL BOARD

Hamilton hit his magical dream card, the Q♣, to make an unbeatable king-high straight flush, the only one ever made at the championship table. He fired $80,000 at the pot and Burgio raised him another $80,000 to put Hamilton all-in if he called. Of course, Hamilton called all in and took down the huge pot.

We cannot know for sure what Burgio held because when Hamilton announced that he had a straight flush, Burgio threw his cards in the muck. This dramatic key hand doubled up Hamilton and put him in position to be a contender the rest of the way. He eventually outlasted runner-up Vincent to win the tournament, with Burgio finishing fourth after this key hand took its toll on his chip stack.

## ACTION HAND 37

### A Draw Outdraws Two Pair
T.J. Cloutier, Commentary

With the ballyhooed return of Stu Ungar, the 1980-81 world champion, to a WSOP final table after a 16-year hiatus, the 1997 WSOP final table was played on a specially built stage surrounded by bleachers on Fremont Street with a full complement of press covering the event. This tournament has become a fabled part of poker lore that players and fans alike still talk about today.

A key hand came up between John Strzemp and Mel Judah when it was still six-handed. The blinds were $5,000/$10,000 with an ante of $2,000. In first position, Judah raised $35,000 holding the A♦ J♠. Strzemp decided to defend his big blind with the 9♣ 7♣, which was somewhat of a marginal call, but he was gambling a little bit to get some chips. The flop came A♣ J♥ 8♣.

Strzemp flopped a flush draw plus an inside straight draw if a 10 came. Judah, of course, flopped top two pair. Strzemp decided to try to steal this pot and moved all-in with his remaining chips. Judah called. Here's how the board looked at the end:

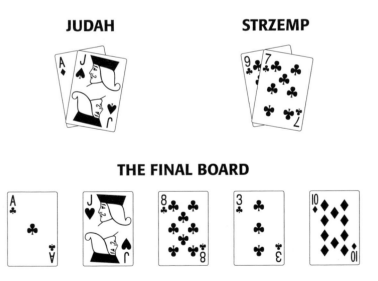

**JUDAH**  **STRZEMP**

**THE FINAL BOARD**

This key hand enabled Strzemp to double up when he hit the flush on the turn card. Of course, even if hadn't made a flush, he still would've won the pot with a straight when the 10 fell on the river. Judah was left short-stacked, although he managed to survive and come back to finish third, while Strzemp went on to finish second to Stu Ungar, who won his third WSOP championship after a 15-year hiatus.

## ACTION HAND 38

### Ungar Sets Up a Bluff in His Final Tournament
T.J. Cloutier, Commentary

In what turned out to be the last time Stu Ungar would play at the WSOP—he died in 1998, the victim of drug abuse—the 1997 WSOP final table was still six-handed when a three-way pot developed between Ungar, Ron Stanley and John Strzemp. Ungar was in the lead with a little more than $1 million in chips, Stanley wasn't far behind in the chip count with $850,000, and Strzemp was in third place. Stanley brought it in for a $45,000 raise, Ungar called on the button, and so did Strzemp in the big blind. The flop came with an ace and a king in it, plus a small card. All three checked on the flop.

On fourth street, a blank came. After Strzemp checked from the blind, Stanley bet $45,000. Ungar called and Strzemp folded. Another raggedy-looking card came off on the river. Stanley checked to Ungar, who value-bet $100,000. As was his habit, Stanley took his time thinking about it before he finally called the bet. Ungar turned over A-Q and scooped in the pot.

The pot had around $300,000 in it, so Ungar lifted a couple hundred thousand off Stanley's stack, which gave him about a 2 to 1 chip lead. Ungar's fairly passive play with A-Q in this key hand milked Stanley out of a big river bet, and set the stage for a later play in which he bluffed him out of a key pot. Champions make these types of plays regularly—they intentionally execute a play to set up another play later in the hand. There is always a method behind their madness.

## ACTION HAND 39

### Getting Pot-Committed

**T.J. Cloutier, Commentary**

A hand came up at the final table of the 1978 World Series of Poker between Jesse Alto and Louis "Sager" Hunsucker that is a good example of what sometimes happens, especially in no-limit hold'em tournaments, when a player who is bluffing or semibluffing decides to call a raise because the pot odds are giving him enough room to justify making the call. In other words, he gets pot-committed.

Hunsucker brought it in for a substantial raise with Q-10 and Alto reraised all-in. Hunsucker would have to commit most of his remaining chips to the pot—he already had one-half of his chips—with what he knew was probably the worst hand. "I know I've got the worst hand," he told Alto. He thought about it, and then he called, saying that since he already had half his chips in the pot, the pot odds on his money for putting the rest of his chips in were at a point that he had to go with the hand. I'm not sure that I would've done it, but I'm not so sure that I wouldn't have done it either. In those days, it wasn't like you were playing for a million bucks, although they were playing for decent money.

When they turned over their hands, Hunsucker found himself up against a hand that he certainly did not want to see—Alto's A-Q. There's more drama to it: The flop came queen-high with connecting straight cards on board. Hunsucker needed to either hit a 10 to make two pair, or hit a gutshot straight card on the river to make a straight with the 10 in his hand.

Guess what? The straight card came and Hunsucker won the pot, sending Alto out in fifth place for a payday of $21,000. Hunsucker hung on for third place and pocketed $63,000, peanuts compared to the $4,517,773 Dennis Phillips took home when he placed third at the 2008 WSOP final table.

## ACTION HAND 40

### The Best Hand Gets the Worst of it
**T.J. Cloutier, Commentary**

Three years after coming second to Bill Smith at the 1985 WSOP, I made the final table for the second time in what turned out to be a classic event. Johnny Chan won his second championship in a row that year, and film of the final hand he played with runner-up Erik Seidel was featured in *Rounders* in 1998.

I thought it was one of the finest tournaments of all time— the final line-up was very tough with Chan, Seidel, Humberto Brenes, Jim Bechtel, Ron Graham, Quentin Nixon, Mike Cox, Jesse Alto, and of course, me. It also was strange in some respects. Every time it was passed to Humberto on the button, he moved in—and I was always in the big blind when he did that. "Sooner or later, I'm gonna pick up a hand," I thought to myself.

The next time Humberto moved all-in on the button, the little blind passed, and I had the A♠ Q♠ in the big blind. I called. He didn't have as many chips as I had. In the stands, his Costa Rican friends were asking him what he had. "Nuevo-six," he answered. I knew how to count in Spanish, so I knew that he'd said he had a 9-6. The flop came 9-6-x, another 9 came on fourth street, and finally a queen came on the end— big deal! Humberto made a full house and knocked me down to almost nothing.

About four hands later when I was on the button, I picked up the A♣ 10♣ and got all-in against Erik, who had 5-5. His fives held up like iron and I went out in fifth place. I thought that it would eventually get down to Chan and Seidel, two great players, and indeed they came first-second. Actually, everybody at the final table was quite a player.

"Catbird" Nixon, who finished seventh, was a terrific player, as was Jesse Alto. Ron Graham, who finished third, had a lot of chips but he never wanted to play a flop—he always moved all his chips into the pot before the flop. Jim Bechtel finished sixth in this one, and went on to win the championship five years later in 1993.

## ACTION HAND 41

### Big Slick Wins a Big Pot
Tom McEvoy, Commentary

In a key hand that turned the tide of the tournament at the 1991 WSOP final table, Robert Veltri opened the betting for $30,000. Brad Daugherty answered the bet by going all-in with the A♣ K♦. Perry Green responded from the blind by going all in with the 8♥ 8♣. Veltri decided to overcall with the J♣ J♥, creating a side pot between him and Green.

| DAUGHERTY | GREEN | VELTRI |
|:---:|:---:|:---:|
|  |  | |

Daugherty was the short stack at this point and if he lost this hand, he would finish fifth. If Veltri won it, he would knock out two players. He was the favorite with two jacks, and he had a lot of chips at that time, but his overcall was marginal, to say the least. The gallery held its breath as the flop, turn and river card were dealt. The final board looked like this:

## THE FINAL BOARD

There were three spades on board but since nobody had spades in his hand, Daugherty's aces won the pot. Veltri won the side pot against Green, sending the Alaskan out in fifth place. In an interview after the hand was over, Green stated that he was very surprised when Veltri called with pocket jacks—it was just too risky against two all-in players. I tend to agree with him, although I still questioned Green's decision to play pockets eights. He apparently played the two eights to try to shut out Veltri and get heads-up against Daugherty, whom he put on two big cards. Green read Daugherty correctly, but he didn't read Veltri right. He thought that he could move Veltri off his hand, but Veltri got stubborn and called, won a substantial side pot, and broke Green.

The problem with Green's play was that Daugherty, a tight player, either had two overcards or a pair bigger than eights. And of course, Green didn't know what Veltri had. He had to have raised with something, and he was yet to act with more chips than Green had. Green knew that Daugherty was very solid, and that against Daugherty alone, he was either a slight favorite or a big underdog if Daugherty had a higher pair. But with Veltri still to act, it was a marginal play. That pot had approximately half a million dollars in it. With 215 players entered in the event, there were $2,150,000 chips in play. After this hand, Daugherty had $500,000 putting him in third place in the chip count, and leading him to the eventual win.

## ACTION HAND 42

### When the Chips Are Down, Count 'Em Up
Tom McEvoy, Commentary

When the play was five-handed at the final table of the 1995 WSOP, it seemed apparent that players were making calls based on the chip counts of their opponents rather than on the strength of their hole cards. In the first scenario, Hamid Dastmalchi was short-stacked against the blinds. On the button he had a suited J-10 and moved in his last chips, $92,000. After the small blind folded, Dan Harrington made a very marginal call in the big blind with a J-3 offsuit. Even with a lot of chips, many pros would not have made that call. He was second in chips at that time, almost tied with Howard Goldfarb. When nothing came to help either hand, Dastmalchi's J-10 won the pot, allowing him to double through Harrington with jack-high, no pair.

In the second scenario, Barbara Enright suffered a truly bad beat. By far the shortest stack, she was in the small blind with 8-8. Enright had just enough chips to make a decent raise. Holding the 6♦ 3♦ in the big blind, Brent Carter called.

## ENRIGHT　　　　　CARTER

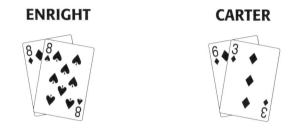

## THE FINAL BOARD

Carter had a lot of chips and he gambled in a spot where a lot of other players would have passed. The board came with the 6♥ 3♠ Q♥ 9♣ A♠, giving Carter two pair and sending the only female player ever to make it to the championship table to the rail. Enright was visibly disappointed at having to settle for fifth place. Her chip count contributed to her defeat just like Dastmalchi's chip count contributed to his doubling up against Hamilton. Enright's ultimate induction into the WSOP Hall of Fame and the Women in Poker Hall of Fame attests to her ability and stature as a world-class poker player.

In scenario three, the blinds were $15,000/$30,000 with three players left. Howard Goldfarb brought it in for a raise on the button, making it $90,000 to go, with the A♥ 4♥. Brent Carter called with the K♠ Q♠. The flop came 8♥ 6♦ 5♥, giving Goldfarb the nut flush draw and an inside straight draw, plus the ace overcard. Carter decided to gamble with his K-Q suited and made a big move-in on Goldfarb. The pot grew to over $600,000. Goldfarb hardly hesitated in calling Carter with what appeared to be a drawing hand.

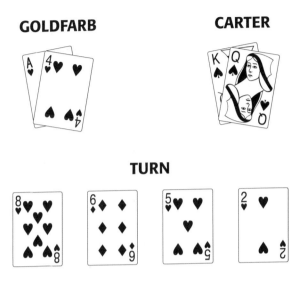

**GOLDFARB**

**CARTER**

**TURN**

A more experienced player might have laid the hand down rather than putting in that much money on a draw heads-up, but as it turned out, Goldfarb's A-4 was a monstrous favorite over Carter's K-Q since Carter had only four cards to pair up that wouldn't also make the flush for his opponent. Carter, of course, was taking a big risk in trying to take Goldfarb off his hand. The turn card was the 2♥ with a blank on the river, giving Goldfarb the nut flush and the pot, and racing Carter out of the tournament in third place.

## ACTION HAND 43

### The Best Kicker Wins a Four-Way Pot

T.J. Cloutier, Commentary

Five-handed at the final table in 2001, the blinds were $15,000/$30,000 with a $6,000 ante. It was costing each player $75,000 a round to sit out. In a hand that combined what Andy Glazer referred to as "comedy, drama, triumph and disaster," Phil Hellmuth limped into the pot, as did Phil Gordon on the button, Carlos Mortensen from the small blind, and Stan Schrier from the big blind, making it a four-way pot. The flop came:

## FLOP

Both blinds checked, Hellmuth bet $60,000, Gordon folded, and Mortensen raised $200,000. After about a two-minute pause, Schrier (who didn't realize it was his turn to act) also folded. It took Hellmuth only about 10 seconds to announce, "I'm all in!" as he pushed his remaining chips to the center of the baize. When Carlos called, he and Phil turned up their cards.

The J♦ on the turn gave Carlos two pair and Phil an open-ended straight draw. He needed either an 8 or a king to make the straight. When the A♠ fell at the end, Phil's $1 million in chips fell into Carlos's stack and the 1989 World Champion of Poker darted out the door in fifth place.

**HELLMUTH**          **MORTENSEN**

## THE FINAL BOARD

This hand is a prime example of how even a great player like Phil Hellmuth can suffer a complete mental block on a hand. As I have written many times in our books, no-limit hold'em is a game of mistakes, and you want to be the player who makes the fewest. Unless you have an extremely big hand after the flop, when you are playing in an unraised pot, you should never—and I stress *never*—give yourself a chance to lose all your chips when you have a decent amount of them to start with.

I see nothing wrong with Phil's original bet of $60,000. He had top pair and was trying to win the pot right there without giving any free cards. But when Carlos raised $200,000, Phil made mistake number one: He called the raise. Why was his call a mistake? Because all he could beat was a bluff. Not only did he call the raise, Phil moved in all his chips against a very good and very aggressive player—mistake number two. Remember that this was an unraised pot. Why would anyone risk losing all his money in this situation?

There are very few hands that Mortensen could have raised with unless he was on a stone bluff. These hands include two overcards and a flush draw, but as this was an unraised pot, you wouldn't consider this hand. Ace-small of spades is one hand that an aggressive player like Mortensen might raise with, but of the drawing hands that he may raise with in this spot, I think that the J♠ 10♠ would be the most likely, in which case he would be favored over one pair. All the other hands (two pair, a small set, K-Q or Q-J) are big favorites over Hellmuth's Q-10.

I believe that if Phil had thought it through before acting, he would not have made mistake number one, let alone mistake number two. All it takes is one major mistake to reduce all of your good play in a tournament to naught and send you home empty handed.

# KEY HANDS AT THE WSOP FINAL TABLE

## 4-HANDED & 3-HANDED

### A Bluff Nixes Two Nines

**T.J. Cloutier, commentary**

A little while after Stu Ungar had won a nice pot with his A-Q at the final table of the 1997 WSOP Main Event, another interesting hand came down that turned out to be the key hand for Ron Stanley. Ungar had inched up a bit further in the lead, but Stanley was still a solid second when a rather innocuous pot developed into something that turned the tide against Stanley.

Stanley limped into the pot from the small blind for $5,000 with the 9♦ 7♦. Ungar had the Q♦ 10♣ in the big blind and checked. The flop came:

**UNGAR**  **STANLEY**

**FLOP**

The flop gave nothing whatsoever to Ungar and a pair of nines to Stanley, who decided to check. Ungar checked behind him. If Stanley had made any kind of bet, it is probable that he would have won the pot right there. The turn card was the 8♣.

Stanley still had a pair of nines with an open-ended straight draw, and Ungar had picked up a gutshot straight draw if a jack hit on the river. Stanley decided to bet $25,000 at the pot. Ungar raised him $60,000 more on a semibluff. If Stanley had an ace in his hand, Ungar couldn't win if he paired either the queen or the 10—he would have to hit a jack to make a straight. Furthermore, a 10 on the river would give Stanley a straight, so Ungar couldn't hit a 10 with safety. He was hoping, of course, that Stanley would fold his hand against his big bet on the turn. Stanley thinks and thinks, and finally calls the $60,000 raise. His call set the stage for the river card.

**UNGAR**                    **STANLEY**

## THE FINAL BOARD

The K♦ didn't help either player, of course, but now there are two overcards on the board to Ron's pair of nines. He checks. Ungar bets $220,000. Ron agonizes at length before he finally folds.

If Ungar hadn't made this big bet, he could not have won the hand in a showdown. After Stanley reluctantly folded, Ungar showed him the bluff by flashing his useless Q-10. Stanley was never the same after that. If he had made the call, he would have been fairly even with Ungar in the chip count and well ahead of the remaining players. Instead, his chip position eroded even further, but more importantly, his confidence also eroded.

## ACTION HAND 45

### A Long Shot Hits the Bulls Eye
T.J. Cloutier, Commentary

A miracle hand unveiled itself at the 1997 Main Event that demonstrates the luck factor in poker. Unfortunately, it also hastened Ron Stanley's ultimate demise at the final table.

With three players left, Stanley brought it in for a raise with the K♦ K♣ and Stu Ungar called. John Strzemp, who was trailing both Ungar and Stanley in the chip count, then decided to move all-in for about $200,000 from the small blind with 10-10. Stanley reraised all in. Ungar folded.

As is the custom when a player is all in, Stanley and Strzemp turned their cards face up. "I folded a 10," Mel Judah announced, meaning that only one 10 was left in the deck. The flop came 3♣ 6♣ 7♠.

Stanley's kings were looking overpowering, and he had a three flush for backup. But amazingly, the turn card was the 10♦—a 44-to-1 shot—followed by the 5♥ on the river to give Strzemp the pot.

### STANLEY          STRZEMP

### THE FINAL BOARD

Stanley looked shocked, devastated. He had already lost a big pot to Ungar, been bluffed out of a pot by Ungar, and now he was beaten by Strzemp's one-outer. This loss dropped Stanley from second to third in the chip count and he went straight downhill from there.

Remember how we talked about how the play of a previous hand often sets the stage for a subsequent hand that either busts you out of the tournament or makes your day? Here is the final, fatal hand for Stanley. Ahead of Stanley in the chip count, Strzemp played it very cagey in the blind with A-A. Stanley made it $60,000 to go preflop with J-8 offsuit, a stone cold bluff on his part—and Strzemp flat called the raise.

When the flop came something like K-7-2 rainbow, Strzemp led at the pot. Apparently deciding that Strzemp was on a bluff just trying to pick up the pot, Stanley moved all-in on him—with no pair, no draw and no hope. Strzemp called and won the pot, busting Stanley out of the tournament in fourth place.

If Stanley hadn't lost the previous series of hands, it is highly unlikely that he would have done what he did—commit poker suicide.

## ACTION HAND 46

### Miss a Bet, Miss a Pot

T.J. Cloutier, Commentary

With Stanley on the rail, three players were left in contention for the 1997 WSOP championship: Stu Ungar, Mel Judah and John Strzemp. Judah opened on the button for $60,000 with a mediocre 10♥ 9♣. Ungar called the raise from the small blind with the Q♦ J♣, and Strzemp folded in the big blind. The flop came J♥ 3♥ 10♦.

Ungar flopped top pair with a reasonable kicker and Judah had second-best pair. Ungar checked the flop and so did Judah. When the 2♣ came on the turn, which didn't help either player, Ungar led $80,000 at the pot. Judah called the bet and raised another $162,000. Ungar called to see the river card, making a huge pot of over $600,000. Here's how the final board looked:

### THE FINAL BOARD

When the K♣ turned up on the river, Judah's tens tanked, giving Ungar's pair of jacks the pot. In this hand, Judah probably should have bet something on the flop just to define his hand. Ungar's bet on fourth street absolutely convinced Judah that Stuey was either on a draw or was bluffing. That had to be true for Judah to make that $162,000 raise with second pair. He still had five outs (two tens and three nines), of course, but he was in terrible shape. Ungar thought before calling the raise—he had entered the pot with a marginal hand to start with, but he had a lot of chips and he wasn't taking a big risk, so his call was correct.

Ungar played beautifully, trapping Judah. At least if Judah had bet the flop, and if Ungar had moved in, Judah probably could've gotten away from his hand. And if Ungar had flat called a bet on the flop, Judah could've shut down the rest of the way and not gone broke to the hand.

Ungar went on to win his third WSOP championship against runner-up Strzemp when he outdrew Strzemp's A-8 with an A-4 by catching a deuce on the river to make a wheel.

It was not the first time that Ungar had won the championship with a wheel. In 1980 he outdrew Doyle Brunson's A♥ 7♥ when he played the 5♠ 4♠. The flop came A-7-2, giving Brunson top two pair and Ungar an inside straight draw. Ungar caught a 3 on fourth street to complete the wheel.

Although Ungar and Johnny Moss both are credited with winning three World Championships of Poker, Ungar is the only player in history who won the title against three full fields of opponents. Moss was voted the title in 1970 and defeated a total of 20 opponents with his wins in 1971 and 1974. Ungar defeated 72 players in 1980, 74 in 1981, and 311 in 1997.

## ACTION HAND 47

### The Draw That Didn't Get There

T.J. Cloutier, Commentary

A key hand came up when it was four-handed at the 1992 final table that put Tom Jacobs in a position to advance to heads-up play for the title against the eventual winner, Hamid Dastmalchi.

With the blinds at $5,000/$10,000, Jacobs brought it in for $30,000 on the button. Both Mike Alsaadi (small blind) and Dastmalchi (big blind) called, making it a $100,000 pot. The flop came K♦ 6♦ 4♣. On a semibluff, Alsaadi moved in with his A♦ J♦ on a flush draw, trying to win it right there. Dastmalchi thought about it and folded. It was Jacobs' turn to think about it. He had opened it preflop for $30,000 with the K♣ J♠, so he had flopped top pair with a mediocre kicker. He decided to call Alsaadi's bet. The flop came K♦ 6♦ 4♣.

When queens came on the turn and river, neither of which was a diamond, Jacobs' two kings won the pot.

**ALSAADI**                    **JACOBS**

**THE FINAL BOARD**

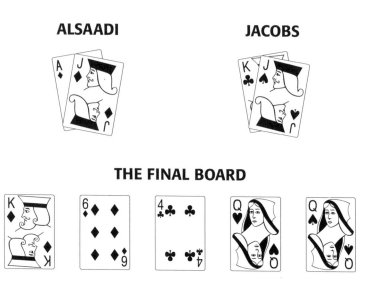

If Jacobs had lost this pot, he would have been crippled and probably would have finished fourth. Instead he won it, and because he had a few more chips than Alsaadi, he sent Alsaadi to the rail in fourth place with a draw that didn't get there.

## ACTION HAND 48

### On Tilt and Off Target

T.J. Cloutier, Commentary

At the 1992 WSOP final table, the play of previous hands set the stage for what Hans "Tuna" Lund did on this hand. Lund had been bluffing and losing regularly. He had been raising, getting reraised, and then folding. After losing a whole series of pots, he probably was on tilt against the one player who was most likely to call him with a marginal hand. That is exactly what Tom Jacobs did.

With the blinds at $10,000/$20,000, Lund had about $175,000 left and moved all in with the 8♣ 7♠. Jacobs called with the K♦ 8♦, which isn't a very good hand, but when matched up against the 8-7 offsuit that Lund held, it was a monster. The flop came:

### JACOBS

### LUND

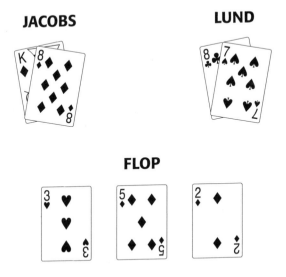

### FLOP

On the turn, Lund caught a 7 to make a pair. Unfortunately for him it was the 7♦, which gave Jacobs the winning flush. This hand put Lund out of the tournament and put Jacobs in a position to later play Dastmalchi heads-up for the title.

If Lund hadn't lost a long series of hands prior to this one, the chances are good that he would not have gone slightly bonkers with his 8-7. In one prior hand Lund misplayed a big pocket pair against Dastmalchi. He didn't bet enough, a misplay that allowed Dastmalchi to hit a set of trips at the river to crack Lund's bigger pair, which also helped set the stage for Lund's downfall. Chip Reese interviewed Lund after he went out, asking him whether he was "a little bit of a hot sucker." Lund answered, "No, not really," adding that if Jacobs won the tournament, he would play him for the whole million later that night. Lund did admit, however, that he had made a mistake on the hand against Dastmalchi.

## ACTION HAND 49

### A Lucky Day for Sevens
Tom McEvoy, Commentary

A pot was played three-handed at the 1994 championship table that was almost unbelievable. Holding the K♥ Q♣, John Spadavecchia opened the pot for a $50,000 raise. Hugh Vincent reraised Spadavecchia $100,000 with the 7♣ 6♣. Russ Hamilton folded and Spadavecchia called the raise. The flop came J♣ 7♦ 10♦, giving Spadavecchia an open-ended straight draw and two overcards, and Vincent a pair of sevens and a three-flush.

Spadavecchia then did something that a lot of seasoned pros would not have done—he checked. Vincent answered the check with a bet of $250,000. With about $550,000 left in chips, Spadavecchia went all-in. Because of the size of the pot, he actually was forcing Vincent to gamble. Vincent decided to accept the challenge—he called the raise.

As the first to act, if Spadavecchia had decided to make an all-in play on the flop, it is doubtful that Vincent could have called him with bottom pair. Calling the check-raise was a very marginal call for Vincent, as was the marginal gambling play by Spadavecchia. But since Spadavecchia had shown some speed to his play, it may be that Vincent thought that he might not have as good a hand as he was representing. The final board looked like this:

### SPADAVECCHIA          VINCENT

## THE FINAL BOARD

When the 2♣ came on the turn, Vincent picked up a flush draw to go with his pair. When the harmless 3♠ showed up on the river, Vincent won a huge pot that put him close to Hamilton in the chip count and eliminated Spadavecchia in third place.

## ACTION HAND 50

### Do Kings Always Beat Jacks?
**T.J. Cloutier, Commentary**

When the action got down to Scotty Nguyen, Kevin McBride and me at the 1998 WSOP final table, I folded pocket jacks twice—and that's hard to do three-handed. Both times Kevin had pocket kings, and both times he played them the same way: He played them slow in the middle position and smooth called a raise. The first time, Scotty brought it in for $40,000, Kevin called, and I reraised. Scotty threw his hand away and Kevin called my raise. The flop came raggedy, I bet, and Kevin came over the top of me. I threw my jacks away in a New York minute and he showed me K-K.

About thirty minutes later, Scotty brought it in for a raise, Kevin called, and again I had J-J. This time I made a smaller raise, and Scotty and Kevin both called. The board came 8-high. "Boy, I wonder if I'm in the same situation again?" I thought. So, I made a little bet at the pot—I didn't want to make a big bet like I had done the time before. Scotty threw his hand away and here comes Kevin over the top again. "Adios, amigos!" I said as I mucked my jacks. Kevin showed me K-K again. Those were two tough laydowns.

On the final hand I played, Kevin raised from the little blind and I reraised him with K-Q in the big blind. I knew that I had the best hand. He called my all-in raise with J♠ 9♠. The flop came with two spades, giving him a flush draw. But instead of another spade, he caught a jack.

I couldn't win with jacks and I couldn't win against them! I was gone in third place in my third final-table appearance.

## ACTION HAND 51

### A Match-Up Made in Heaven?
**T.J. Cloutier, Commentary**

"It was a match-up made in poker heaven," the tournament reporter wrote about the 2001 WSOP $2,000 no-limit hold'em tournament. "Phil Hellmuth, the 1989 WSOP champ with six bracelets in 25 finishes versus T.J. Cloutier, the all-time tournament money winner with 33 finishes. Layne Flack, who finished third, also brought two bracelets to the table and Steve Rydel added one more."

When Hellmuth and I got heads-up for the title, he had nearly a 3 to 1 edge over me in chips. When somebody asked me for a chip count, I replied, "Slightly lopsided." But as often happens, the key hand at the final table was not played heads-up between the two finalists—it happened earlier when Hellmuth beat Layne Flack in an unraised pot when it was down to three players. At the time, we were all about even in chips. I was not in the hand—Hellmuth and Flack played it heads-up. Here is my re-creation of the flop (although I don't recall the exact suits of the cards, I clearly recall the ranks). I'm not showing Flack's hole cards because he never turned them up, and pocket cams were not yet used in tournaments.

## HELLMUTH          FLACK

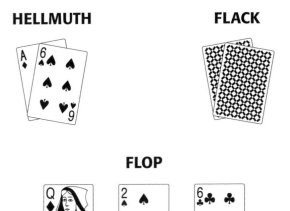

## FLOP

Here's how it happened: After the original bring-in and call, the flop came Q-2-6 rainbow, giving Hellmuth a pair of sixes. Hellmuth checked and Flack checked behind him. When a 9 came on fourth street, Hellmuth made a bet of about $25,000 and Flack raised $50,000 more. Thinking that Flack was bluffing, Hellmuth called the raise. Fifth street brought another 6, so the final board looked like this:

## HELLMUTH          FLACK

## THE FINAL BOARD

When Flack moved all-in, Hellmuth finally realized that he must have had a hand when he raised on fourth street. However, unless Flack had filled at the river—maybe he was holding pocket queens—Hellmuth knew that he had the best hand with trip sixes and an ace kicker. He called Flack's all-in bet and won the pot.

Catching that third 6 was the key moment at the final table. When Hellmuth turned over his A-6, Flack quietly mucked his cards face down and walked out the door in third place. Later that day, he confided to me that he had slow-played pocket kings in the hope of trapping Hellmuth.

Flack had played it perfectly. But no matter how well—or sometimes how badly—you play a hand, Lady Luck has a big say in no-limit hold'em.

## ACTION HAND 52

### Kings Win a King's Ransom
Tom McEvoy, Commentary

When it got to three-handed play at the 1981 WSOP championship table, Perry Green had a substantial chip lead. Stu Ungar, the defending champion, was a solid second, and Gene Fisher was trailing as a distant third. There were 75 players that year with $750,000 worth of chips in play.

Green was on the button holding the A♠ Q♦ and opened the pot for $80,000. Clearly he overbet the pot. Sitting on $200,000 in the big blind, Stu Ungar called the $80,000 and raised $120,000 more with K♠ K♥, putting himself all-in. If Green hadn't overbet the pot to start with, there's a chance that he might have considered backing off—but he had committed a lot of chips at this point, and didn't hesitate very long in calling.

In a nutshell, here's why the outcome of this hand was so important: If Green wins this pot, he probably will have 90 percent of the chips and will get heads-up with Fisher for the title. If Ungar wins the pot, Green is still a solid second in chips, but Ungar will have over one-half the chips in play and will be the chip leader. The flop came A♣ 5♦ 10♦.

With all the money in before the flop, Green and Ungar turned their cards face up. Green had flopped an ace, which gave him top pair and reduced Ungar to two outs to win the hand. He caught one of them on fourth street, the K♦, giving him trip kings. However Green now had a flush draw and an inside-straight draw, so he had some redraws to the nuts. But he missed them all when the 4♣ fell on the river.

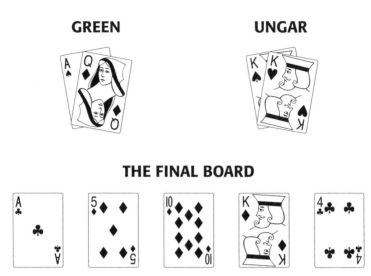

**GREEN**

**UNGAR**

**THE FINAL BOARD**

Winning this hand was the turning point for Stu Ungar as it gave him the lead. If Ungar hadn't won this one—after the ace flopped, he became a big dog to the hand—he couldn't have won the tournament. Indeed it was a dramatic hand to watch.

## ACTION HAND 53

### A Set Outlasts a Draw
Tom McEvoy, Commentary

The third-place finisher to Rod Peate and me at the 1983 WSOP championship table was the legendary Doyle Brunson, who already had won back-to-back championships in 1976-77. In 1980 against the rookie Stu Ungar, he came in second, so with the possible exception of Amarillo Slim, Doyle was the most famous poker player in the world at that time.

Three-handed Doyle played a hand against Rod and got himself broke. Rod raised on the button with 9-9. Doyle called the raise from the small blind with the J♦ 9♦. I folded my big blind. The flop came 9-high with two diamonds, giving Doyle top pair and a flush draw, which looked pretty good on the surface. The only problem was that he was up against Rod's set of nines.

Doyle checked the flop and Rod bet around $15,000. Doyle moved all-in with over a quarter-million in chips. He overbet the pot, apparently trying to run over Rod. But Rod had bet about $9,000 before the flop, and had made it $15,000 to go on the flop, so he wasn't about to relinquish the hand. He called the all-in bet. When no diamond came to rescue Doyle from defeat, the legend joined his many fans on the rail, and Rod and I began a long heads-up duel to the finish.

## ACTION HAND 54

### A Famous Bluff Goes Down in History
Dana Smith, Commentary

Byron "Cowboy" Wolford pulled off one of the most dramatic bluffs in WSOP history at the final table of the 1984 championship event. Few people remember the final hand that Keller and Wolford played for the title, but almost every tournament aficionado remembers this key hand.

The action was down to three players, Cowboy Wolford, Jack Keller, and Jesse Alto (who had the chip lead) when this hand came up. Before the flop, Keller folded on the button, Wolford flat called from the small blind and Alto checked in the big blind.

The flop came A♣ 9♣ K♦. Wolford bet $15,000 and Alto called. On the turn came the K♥. Wolford sent $40,000 into the pot and again Alto called. When the 2♥ came at the river, Wolford pushed in all his chips, about $101,000. Alto thought for a long time before finally folding his hand face down, so we don't know what cards he had. The chances are good, however, that he had a far better hand than Wolford's 5-3, which the Texas cowboy flashed.

This key hand turned the tide of fortune between the three finalists. Apparently on tilt from succumbing to Wolford's start-to-finish bluff, Alto threw off the rest of his stack to Jack Keller, the eventual champion, promoting Wolford to second place and demoting himself to third. The cowboy told me in our interview years later that he had planned to bluff Alto from the get-go, since he knew from playing with him in road games that Jesse always steamed when he lost a big hand. "He never did know how to keep a cool head at the poker table," Wolford said.

The 1984 WSOP was unique in that it is the only year they played with actual money. The chips were exchanged for cash at the final table when it got down to three players. Hundred-dollar bills wrapped in bundles of $50,000 rolled across the table like ping pong balls as Keller, Alto and Wolford bet back and forth. These days it probably would take million-dollar bundles of money to play real cash in three-handed action.

## ACTION HAND 55

### Overbetting the Pot Backfires
Dana Smith, Commentary

The hand that gave eventual winner Johnny Chan the lead for good at the 1987 WSOP final table came down when it was three-handed. At that time Bob Ciaffone was in the lead, Chan was second, and Frank Henderson was a distant third. Basically, Ciaffone overbet the pot twice—that is, the blinds were relatively small in relation to the size of his bets—and got himself in over his head when he decided to gamble to try to draw out.

Here's the way the play came down: With the ante at $2,000 and the blinds at $10,000/$20,000, Ciaffone picked up the A♦ 4♦ in the big blind. Chan called on the button with the K♥ Q♥ and Henderson also called from the small blind. Ciaffone then raised $85,000 more, overbetting the pot. To Ciaffone's surprise, Chan called his big raise. Henderson passed. Down came the flop:

**CHAN**

**CIAFFONE**

**FLOP**

Chan made top pair and Ciaffone made bottom pair. Ciaffone led at the pot for $185,000, his second overbet, and Chan moved all-in with a $240,000 raise. With two face cards on board, Ciaffone went into the think tank and after a long deliberation, he called. "It seemed remote that Chan would be on a draw," Ciaffone wrote in *Pot-Limit & No-Limit Poker*, "but it looked like an ace or a 4 would win the pot for me, and make me a huge favorite to become the world champion. Since I was almost getting the right odds, and would still be in the hunt if I lost the pot, I called the raise." With no help on the turn or river, Ciaffone lost the pot and Chan took the lead at the final table.

Admittedly, Ciaffone did not want to play Chan heads-up. This probably is the reason why he overbet the pot on the flop to try to get Chan to lay down the hand. He could've still folded the hand, of course, when Chan came over the top of him. "I should have checked that flop," Ciaffone wrote in retrospect, "but it only takes one mistake to cost you a tournament—and the title of world champion. Even so, my experiences at the final table were the greatest thrill in my life."

Later on, Ciaffone went broke with 7♠ 5♠ when he flopped middle pair and a flush draw against Chan's top pair-top kicker. Chan had A-J and the flop came jack high. Henderson, who was in last place with 24 players left in action, had come to the final table dead last in chips. He slowly climbed the money ladder and finished second to Chan by playing a sound survival strategy.

# ♠ 13
# HEADS-UP AT THE WSOP FINAL TABLE

## ACTION HAND 56

### A Big Bluff Turns the Tide

T.J. Cloutier, Commentary

When he was about 28 years old, Bobby Baldwin was considered to be the best no-limit hold'em player alive. All-time great Bobby Hoff once said that Baldwin was 15 percent better than anybody playing poker at that time. During the 1978 World Series of Poker, Baldwin and Crandell Addington were playing heads-up for the title when Baldwin pulled off a successful bluff that changed the entire course of the tournament. Although it was not the final hand, this was the key hand because it shifted the momentum of the final-table play.

Addington had the lead at this point. With the blinds at $3,000/$6,000, he raised $10,000. We don't know what his cards were, but we do know that Baldwin called the raise with 10-9 offsuit. People don't realize that a lot of times, hands are played *before* the players ever see a flop. That is, a player decides in advance how he's going to play a hand, no matter what. So, when Baldwin called Addington's raise with a 10-9, he probably had it in his mind that even if he didn't get a great flop to his hand, he was going to win the pot anyway. Long before the flop actually came up, Baldwin had decided that he was going to make a move on this pot.

The flop came Q-3-4 with two diamonds and Baldwin led at it for a substantial amount. Addington called. Off came the A♦ on the turn, putting three diamonds on the board. Baldwin moved in. Baldwin seized his opportunity. You've heard me say a million times that you must have balls of iron to play no-limit hold'em—you have to be willing to sacrifice everything you have on a major bluff. And Baldwin was such a good player that he didn't think twice about it. Even though Addington had called him on the flop, Baldwin moved on it when the board came with something that he could represent.

What if the turn card had been a brick? In that case Baldwin would have shut down. He would have taken his loss with the hand because he knew that Addington had a hand when he called him on the flop. Realize, too, that when Baldwin moved in on the turn, Addington could have had two diamonds in his hand, but that was the chance that Baldwin had to take. Since Addington had raised before the flop, there's a chance that he had a pair or a "big ace," and that he did not have any diamonds in his hand, in which case Baldwin's power play would work.

When an ace came on the turn, if Addington had put Baldwin on a flush, he would not have called even if he had a big ace—but he would've taken more time to muck his hand. As it happened, he threw it away quickly, so the chances are that he did not have a big ace. Baldwin flashed his cards as he scooped in the pot, but we'll never know what Addington's cards were.

This successful bluff changed the tide of events at the final table. If Addington had called, the tournament would have been over because Baldwin probably had no outs if, for example, Addington had a queen. And Addington would have had what he coveted as much as all the money he had earned from the oil business, which was very substantial. He would have won the World Series of Poker championship.

## ACTION HAND 57
### Flushed Out on the River
**T.J. Cloutier, Commentary**

Before this key hand unraveled at the 1979 WSOP final table, professional Bobby Hoff had about a 3 to 2 chip lead on amateur Hal Fowler. Hoff had a little over $300,00 and Fowler had a little more than $200,000 of the $540,000 chips in play. Hoff had the K♦ 6♦ on the button and Fowler held the A♦ 8♦. Hoff raised before the flop and Fowler called. The flop came 9♣ J♥ 7♦.

The flop gave Hoff nothing except an overcard and it gave Fowler an inside-straight draw. Fowler checked the flop, Hoff led with a $25,000 bet, and Fowler called drawing to his inside straight and a three-flush with an ace overcard. We called Fowler "Mr. Inside Straight" at this World Series because he consistently drew to inside straights at the final table in particular and made an amazing number of them.

The 2♦ came on fourth street giving both Fowler and Hoff a backdoor flush draw. Fowler checked and Hoff bet $30,000, not a huge bet. Without hesitating, Fowler called with his middle-buster straight draw, an overcard, and the nut flush draw—a big draw to try to make with one card to come.

The river card was the Q♦, which made the flush for both of them.

**FOWLER**                    **HOFF**

## THE FINAL BOARD

When the Q♦ came on the river, Fowler did not check—he moved in with his remaining $144,000. Hoff studied the situation, hesitating for a while, although his hesitation was more for the audience than anything else. At this point there was $298,000 in chips in the pot of the $540,000 in play. Hoff had backdoored the second nuts—naturally, he thought he had the winner, so he called the bet, only to see his arch rival turn over the nuts.

It is surprising that Fowler checked the hand twice and then led with it for all his chips. You would think that once he had made the nuts, if he thought that Hoff would bet, he would have checked to him. Of course, Hoff had the chip lead and was being the aggressor, but he was out on a limb—he had started by trying to steal the pot and wound up making the hand, only to get it cracked. This hand actually turned the Main Event around and put Fowler in the lead for the rest of the tournament.

There were 54 players in this tournament. If they were giving odds on the favorite and the favorite was even money,

Fowler would have been 54 to 1 to win it, the longest shot in the whole event. And now he had the chip lead at the final table heads-up, which just shows that anybody can do it. On the videotape, Hal said that he had been playing poker for 42 years and had played hold'em for eight years. Although he was an amateur tournament player, at least he understood the basics of the game—and got lucky.

## ACTION HAND 58

### Pocket Aces Against a Draw
**T.J. Cloutier, Commentary**

The final hand at the 1979 WSOP was a classic. Bobby Hoff had $121,000 and Hal Fowler had $419,000. Holding A-A, Hoff raised, making it $38,000 to play. Most players in Fowler's situation—he had a 4 to 1 lead—would look for a premium hand to play to try to grind a man out in this spot, and he certainly would not play a pot with a weak hand when the other man had raised. But Hal didn't play it that way—he called the raise with 7-6 offsuit, making it a $76,000 pot. Although that is not how most professionals would play when they had a big chip lead, being the amateur that he claimed to be, Hal played any two cards.

The flop came J-5-3. Bobby bet $40,000 and Hal called with an inside-straight draw. Since he had called $38,000 before the flop, it seems a cinch that he was going to call $40,000 on the flop with a middle-buster straight draw and the chip lead. It's rare that you would even get a flop that you would have a draw to with 7-6 offsuit. But now Fowler had a chance to bust Hoff if he caught the right card. Of course, off came a 4 on fourth street. He checked and Hoff bet $43,000 all-in. Naturally Fowler called. He had made the nuts and sent Hoff and his pocket rockets to the rail in second place.

Hoff probably would not have lost this pot if he had been playing against a more experienced, better player because with that big a lead, a world-class player would not have played the pot with him. If you have a 4 to 1 lead on somebody, you don't want to play big pots, all you want to do is grind them out. Why give the other guy a chance to catch up? If you have $400,000 and he has $100,000, why would you want to let things get to where it's 3 to 2, meaning that if you lose one pot you will be behind.

Although Fowler didn't understand tournament strategy, he knew how to play the hand once he had made the call, so he was no rank amateur. Once he picked up the draw, he knew that Hoff couldn't break him, so he called $40,000 on the flop to make the straight. Then he was smart enough to check it on the turn. But it actually didn't matter whether he checked or bet—Hoff was going to call anyway if Fowler led at the pot.

Fowler's reaction when he won the title was amazing—he just sat there like a mannequin. One commentator attributed his lack of enthusiasm to the apparently large number of Valiums or Qualudes that he had consumed to calm his nerves.

## ACTION HAND 59

### Tripped Up by Jacks Heads-Up
Tom McEvoy, Commentary

At the 1981 WSOP championship table, the lead had seesawed back and forth several times between Stu Ungar and Perry Green, which was one of the fascinating things about this final table. Green was in the lead when this hand happened. Perry was a very aggressive player, as was Stu, and both these guys put in all their money on either premium hands or drawing hands.

Perry had the chip lead when he got involved with the 10♣ 2♣ on the button against Stu's A♣ J♣. The flop came J♦ 9♣ 8♣.

Stu flopped top pair with the nut flush draw, and Perry flopped a flush draw plus an open-ended straight draw. After going to war raising back and forth, Perry moved in on Stu. If Perry wins this hand, the tournament is over. If Stu wins the hand, he will have a substantial chip lead. There was $554,000 in the pot out of $750,000 chips in play, the biggest pot ever played at a WSOP tournament to that date.

That Perry had this much gamble to him in this spot is interesting. He could've just called Stu's bet and tried to make his hand cheaply, but instead he decided to go to war with him right on the flop—but Stu decided not to lay down top pair and the nut flush draw. Here's how the board looked at the end:

### UNGAR          GREEN

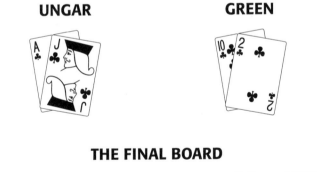

### THE FINAL BOARD

When the J♠ came on the turn, Stu made trip jacks. Only a straight card on the river would save Perry, but it didn't show up. Stu won the pot and took the chip lead. Later in the event, Perry rallied to make another comeback, though to no avail.

## ACTION HAND 60

### Draw Against Draw for the Bracelet
Tom McEvoy, Commentary

In the last hand of the 1981 WSOP final table when the blinds were $4,000/8,000, Green and Ungar went to the center with drawing hands. On the button with 10♣ 9♦, Green made it $16,000 to go, a modest raise. Ungar was looking down at the A♥ Q♥ and reraised $25,000 more. Green made a very marginal play when he called the raise. The flop came:

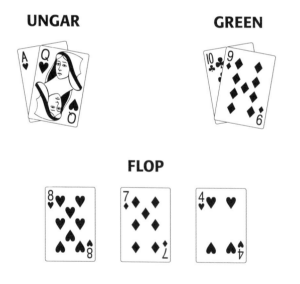

**UNGAR**            **GREEN**

**FLOP**

Ungar flopped the nut flush draw and Green had an open-ended straight draw with two overcards. Ungar went for the kill—he bet $100,000. Green called with his last $78,000 in chips. The way the betting went was rather interesting. Without hesitation, Stu moved in—and without hesitation, Green called.

The pot had well over $200,000 in it, which was close to one-third of the total chips in play. If Green won the pot, it would put him back into a competitive position, although he still would not have had the lead. The 4♣ paired the board on the turn, but didn't help either one of them. The Q♦ on the river paired Ungar, although it didn't alter the outcome because he would've won the pot anyway with ace-high.

### UNGAR           GREEN

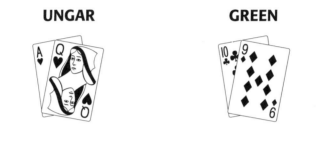

### THE FINAL BOARD

During this tournament, Ungar and Green played three key hands against each other, all of which Ungar won—Ungar's K-K against Green's A-Q when an ace flopped and a king came on the turn; Ungar's A♣ J♣ against Green's 10♣ 2♣; and the final hand.

Green had been incredibly lucky against the other players, however. When he hit a two-outer to make a bigger set against Baldwin's set, Green would have been eliminated if Baldwin had won the pot and Baldwin would have become the chip leader, so the entire course of the tournament was affected. Ungar was lucky to have his hands win against Green, and

Green was lucky to have his hands win against some of the other players. Skill and luck is a powerful combination in tournament action.

## ACTION HAND 61

### Queens Win a 7-Hour Marathon
Tom McEvoy, Commentary

Rod Peate and I had been playing heads-up at the 1983 WSOP championship table for seven hours when the final hand came up. The blinds were $8,000/$16,000 and Rod raised $40,000 on the button with K-J suited. I hadn't been dealt one big pocket pair all day long and here I was looking down at Q-Q. "I'm all-in!" I announced. Everybody sensed that the end was finally near.

Rod didn't take a lot of time to call, which surprised me. In hindsight, of course, he has regretted his hasty decision, but at the time he was exhausted. I had been playing to try to wear him down and, basically, that plan had been working. I think he just snapped. His rationale in calling my all-in bet probably was, "What if Tom has something like two nines? I still have two overcards."

The flop came 6-6-3. Rod hit a jack on the turn, giving him jacks and sixes. The river card was another three. Rod would have regained the lead if he had been able to draw out on my queens (the pot was over $600,000), although that didn't necessarily mean that he would have won the tournament. When my two queens held up, I jumped up from my seat with my arms raised in victory—it was the thrill of my life! Rod and I also made WSOP history as the first satellite winners to appear at the championship table.

## ACTION HAND 62

### Lucky in a Key Hand, Unlucky in the Final Hand
**T.J. Cloutier, Commentary**

When Bill Smith, Berry Johnston and I were playing three-handed at the championship table of the 1985 WSOP, I got very lucky against Berry in a key hand. Berry raised the pot with A-K offsuit and I called with the A♥ J♥. When the board came K-J-2, Berry bet and I called with second-best pair. Then on the turn, off came another jack, sending Berry to the rail in third place. Finally I had gotten lucky against someone at the final table!

Bill Smith and I used to play the Southern Circuit together and had been close friends for years. Everybody knows that Bill was an alcoholic, and by the time we got to heads-up play, he was just starting to feel the booze. You could always tell when Bill was drunk because he would start calling the flop. If it came 10-7-4, he would say, "21!" And if he had to leave the table for a bathroom break, he'd have a little hop in his step. We used to call it a "git-up in his git-along."

When Bill and I started heads-up play, I had the most chips. Then a key hand came up in which I had 9-9 and he had K-K. I raised and he reraised. Bill won the pot and took a big lead over me. Then I started chipping away at him and got to the point where I had one-quarter of the chips and he had three-quarters—Bill was drinking heavily and that made it easy to get his chips. When he was sober, he was the tightest player in the world. When he was half-drunk, he might've been the best player in the world. And when he was drunk, he was horrible. And he was getting to that point.

I had just won a pot with something like a 5-4 suited when I looked down at an ace. Bill raised it and I moved in with my whole stack. I didn't even look at my second card because there was a chance that I could win it with a raise, or if not, I'd probably have the best hand anyway, two overcards if he had a pair. My chances were pretty good.

Bill called my all-in bet and turned over 3-3. That's when I looked at my kicker for the first time—it was a 3! I only had one overcard against his pair. The flop came 4-5-10, so I could have caught an ace or a deuce after the flop to make a straight. But that didn't happen and my good friend Bill won the title. This was the first of two years that I came in second for the championship. I'll tell you about the second time a little later.

## ACTION HAND 63

### From Rags to Riches
Tom McEvoy, Commentary

In 1990 Hans "Tuna" Lund faced off against Mansour Matloubi for the WSOP championship, the cash and the bracelet. The blinds were quite high, $15,000/$30,000. On the button Lund went all in with pocket fours for about $300,000. Matloubi called with pocket sixes, so the pot was close to $700,000 in chips. Matloubi had a substantial chip lead, so Lund definitely was in trouble going into this hand.

If Lund had won this hand, he would have been back in contention for the title although he still would have been trailing in the chip count. He would have been competitive at least. The flop came 8-Q-2 with no help for either player on the turn and river. Mansour won the championship with a pair of sixes.

The highlight of the match-up between winner Matloubi and runner-up Lund, however, was not the final hand—it was a hand that occurred shortly before the showdown. On the button, Matloubi brought it in for a $75,000 raise with pocket tens. Lund, who was in the chip lead, called the raise with A♣ 9♦. The flop came 9♠ 2♣ 4♦, giving Lund top pair and top kicker, and Matloubi an overpair to the flop.

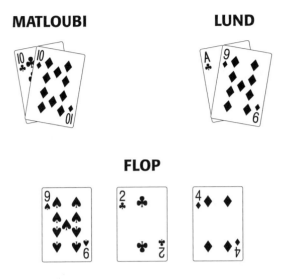

Lund checked, Matloubi led off with a $100,000 bet, and Lund raised $250,000 more. Matloubi studied and thought. Finally he called the $250,000 raise and reraised the rest of his chips, $378,000. It was Lund's turn to study and think. After a long pause, he shrugged his shoulders and called the raise. I think Lund knew that he was beaten at this point, but he had already invested so much money in the pot he just decided to go for it.

In one of the most dramatic hands in WSOP history, the A♠ hit on the turn, giving Lund the lead with two pair, aces and nines, against Matloubi's pocket tens. Matloubi had only two outs to win the pot, the two tens left in the deck, which was a 22 to 1 shot. There were 44 unseen cards—two of them would give Matloubi the winning hand and 42 were losers for him. He was in a world of hurt.

When the ace hit on fourth street, Matloubi paced around the table nervously and actually kicked his chair. With all the money in, Lund had Matloubi covered and would become the world champion unless a two-outer 10 fell on the river. And that is exactly what happened!

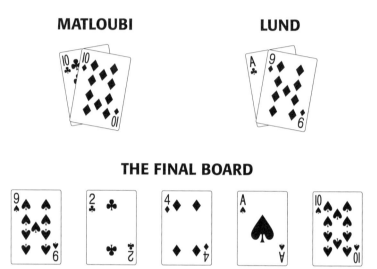

**MATLOUBI**          **LUND**

**THE FINAL BOARD**

When the miracle 10♠ came on the river, Matloubi won the pot, which had over 80 percent of the chips in it. Indeed it was a rags-to-riches story for Matloubi: He literally went from imminent elimination to the chip lead and the eventual title. It was a far different story for Lund, who sat motionless and mute, crestfallen over losing the hand.

This key hand was exciting to watch because the lead kept switching back and forth. Lund probably would not have gone broke with pocket fours on the final hand if he had not been forced to play a hand after his loss to Matloubi in this hand—but the blinds were so high that he had to take a stand with something.

"This is the most incredible hand in WSOP history," the announcer remarked. Certainly it was one of the most dramatic flip-flop hands I've ever seen.

## *ACTION HAND 64*

### A Gutshot Draw Gets Shot Down

Tom McEvoy, Commentary

In the final hand of the 1991 WSOP Main Event, Don Holt limped on the button with the 7♥ 3♥. Holding the K♠ J♠, Daugherty raised $75,000 more. Holt made a minor mistake by limping on the button, although it wasn't terrible because it only cost him half a bet and he had position. Calling Daugherty's raise was Holt's big mistake.

The 8-9-J flop gave Daugherty top pair and Holt a three-flush with a gutshot straight draw (a 10 would make a straight for him). Of course, if Daugherty had a queen in his hand, the 10 would give him an even higher straight.

Daugherty checked the flop and Holt moved in for about $450,000. I think this was a bad play on Don's part because an 8-9-J flop can hit people in a lot of different ways, making it a dangerous flop to go up against. Nonetheless, here they were playing another million-dollar pot!

**DAUGHERTY**

**HOLT**

**THE FINAL BOARD**

This time, however, Daugherty had the chip lead going in. He didn't take much time to call Holt's semibluff. The 5♣ on the turn gave Holt eight outs to hit a straight (a 6 or a 10 would do it for him). But when the 8♠ came on the river, his drawing days were over and Daugherty became the 1991 world champion—and the first million-dollar winner at the WSOP.

Holt picked the wrong time to put all his chips in on an inside-straight draw. It is dangerous to bluff at a coordinated flop because people will catch a part of it, especially when cards such as J-10 or J-9 come on the flop, and make a play at the pot. And that is exactly what happened in the final hand between Daugherty and Holt. Daugherty had been far outchipped at one point and made a tremendous comeback to win the title.

## ACTION HAND 65

### Marginal Hands Vie for Victory
Tom McEvoy, Commentary

Sometimes, all the money goes in with some rather marginal hands. That's what happened in the final hand of the 1992 WSOP championship match between Hamid Dastmalchi and Tom Jacobs. Don't forget, however, that when you're playing heads-up, the value and strength of hands changes. Because only two players are contesting each pot, it takes less strength to play a hand. Therefore, you can play more marginal hands than you ordinarily would—which is exactly what happened in this scenario.

In my opinion, Jacobs misplayed this final hand. Take a look at my analysis and see whether you agree with me. With a little over $2 million in chips in play, Dastmalchi had about a 2 to 1 chip lead. The blinds were $10,000/$20,000 with a $2,000 ante. Dastmalchi held 8-4 offsuit and Jacobs held J-7 offsuit, not very good starting hands to say the least. Jacobs called to see the flop for $10,000 on the button (the button is the small blind in heads-up in tournament play), and Dastmalchi checked rather than raising. The flop came J♥ 5♦ 7♦.

Jacobs flopped top two pair and a three-flush. Dastmalchi had no diamonds, and needed a 6 to make an inside straight. How would you bet Jacobs' hand on the flop?

With $2 million in chips in play and over $600,000 in his stack, Jacobs only bet $30,000 into this $44,000 pot. He apparently underbet the pot trying to lure Dastmalchi into it, which is where I think he made a mistake. With two diamonds and two connecting cards on board, there was a lot of drawing potential on this flop, especially in an unraised pot. I believe he should have made a bigger bet, at least $50,000 or $60,000. Dastmalchi called.

Obviously, if Jacobs had raised before the flop, Dastmalchi probably would have folded. But on the flop, even though he was only drawing to an inside straight, $30,000 was a minimal chip investment for Dastmalchi compared to the huge implied odds the pot was offering him. In other words, by limping in before the flop and then underbetting on the flop, Jacobs had let him in too cheap. Dastmalchi knew that if he hit his hand, he would have a very good chance of busting Jacobs. And that's exactly what happened.

**DASTMALCHI**          **JACOBS**

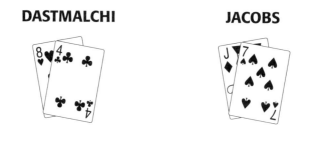

## THE FINAL BOARD

When the 6♥ peeled off on the turn, Dastmalchi checked his straight, which I think was the correct play. Jacobs moved his $600,000 all-in, overbetting the pot instead of underbetting it with a connecting card on board. This was his second mistake.

Evidently he was trying to shut Dastmalchi out in case he was on a draw. (Of course, he already had made his draw). When the 8♣ fell on the river, Dastmalchi's hand held up and his arms shot up in victory as he became the 1992 WSOP world champion of poker.

In the next Action Hand, I discuss a mistake that another world-class player made at the final table of the WSOP Main Event.

## ACTION HAND 66

### Three Ladies Beat a Belly Buster
Tom McEvoy, Commentary

When the play was heads-up between Hugh Vincent and Russ Hamilton at the 1994 WSOP championship table, another incredible hand unveiled itself. At this point Vincent had the lead with about $1,600,000 in chips and Hamilton had $1,070,000. Hamilton brought it in for $150,000 with the Q♣ Q♠. Vincent called the raise with a 10-9 offsuit, a marginal hand for that size of bet.

The flop comes Q♥ 6♦ 5♥, giving Hamilton top set and Vincent nothing. Hamilton correctly checks the flop, trying to trap Vincent into some sort of action. Vincent doesn't take the bait and checks behind him. Then comes the 8♠ on fourth street. Vincent now has a double-belly-buster straight draw—he can make a straight with either a jack or a 7. Hamilton fires $400,000 at this pot, leaving half a million in chips in reserve. At this point he had a little more than one-half of his chips in the pot.

Now comes the part where Vincent misplayed his hand. Although Vincent had an out to make his hand, it was apparent that Hamilton was pretty well pot-committed. All Vincent had on the turn was a 10-high hand with one card to come—and he decided to move in on Hamilton, a very questionable play. Since Hamilton had so many chips already in the pot, Vincent had to realize that there was a pretty good chance that he was going to call, which he did.

The board paired on the end with the 8♣, giving Hamilton a full house, a giant pot, and the chip lead. Vincent's stack was reduced to around half a million in chips. This $2 million pot was a WSOP record at that time.

## ACTION HAND 67

### Eights Were Looking Great
Tom McEvoy, Commentary

Dan Harrington had a pretty substantial chip lead when the final hand came down against Howard Goldfarb at the 1995 WSOP championship table. On the button with A♥ 7♣, Goldfarb looked to be a favorite preflop over whatever

Harrington was holding. With the blinds at $15,000/$30,000, he made a $100,000 bring-in bet. Harrington decided to gamble with the 9♦ 8♦ and called the raise. Goldfarb still had over $600,000 left, which was a substantial amount of chips.

When the flop came 8-6-2, Harrington made a pair of eights. He checked and Goldfarb moved his entire $600,000 into the pot. Without too much hesitation, Harrington called him with top pair and a mediocre kicker. There were a lot of hands that Goldfarb could have held that would have beaten Harrington, or he could even have had a strong draw—but basically, he was in there on a total bluff after the flop. Here's what happened to his grand bluff:

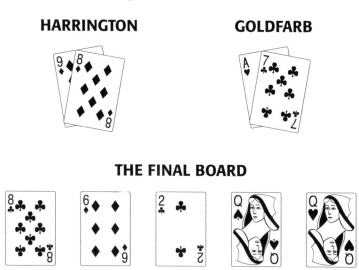

### HARRINGTON      GOLDFARB

### THE FINAL BOARD

The queens on the turn and river helped neither player. Harrington won the hand—and the championship—with a pair of eights. Primarily a cash-game player prior to 1995, Harrington honed his tournament skills and went on to make back-to-back final tables at the WSOP Main Event, placing third behind Chris Moneymaker in 2003, and fourth to Greg Raymer in 2004.

## ACTION HAND 68

### Quads Over Quads at the WSOP

**T.J. Cloutier, Commentary**

Layne Flack won his first big tournament at the Rio Carnivale of Poker in the mid '90s. The tournament poker world was much smaller then, more like a high school reunion than a big convention of strangers like it is today. Since then he's won six gold bracelets and has earned the nickname "Back to Back Flack" by winning two of them at the 2002 WSOP. Here's how it came about.

In his first gold bracelet win in 2002, he faced Tom Jacobs at the final table of the $2,000 no-limit hold'em event. With the chip lead, Flack raised preflop with the K♥ Q♣ and Jacobs called with the K♠ 10♣. On the K♦ Q♠ 7♠ flop, Jacobs sent his entire stack to the middle with top pair and a three flush. Naturally, Flack covered the bet with top two pair and took down the title when Jacobs got no further help.

Flack then entered the next no-limit hold'em tournament, the $1,500 event. Like the final table I told you about in 2001 (Action Hand 51), we again had an outstanding field: Flack, Philip Marmorstein, Carlos Mortensen, Johnny Chan and I were the final five. That's when Flack and Marmorstein played one of the most incredible final-table hands I've ever witnessed.

In this key hand, Flack went to battle heads-up with the 10♦ 10♥ and the chip lead over Marmorstein, who held the 4♥ 4♣. The flop came 10♠ 10♣ 8♣.

Can you believe this? Layne flopped quads! Slowplaying them, he checked to Phil, who also checked. As fate would have it, Phil got just enough help on the turn to believe he stood a chance of winning the pot with fours full of tens.

On the turn, Layne underbet the pot, pushing $15,000 to the middle. Phil called. And guess what? He made quads on the river when the case 4 hit the board! When Layne pushed all-in, Phil followed suit of course.

### FLACK          MARMORSTEIN

### THE FINAL BOARD

Can you imagine the exhilaration Phil must have felt when he saw that river card? And his total devastation when he got knocked out of the tournament with quads?

I went out in third place when I played an A-Q against Layne and Johnny. Wouldn't you know, they both had A-K! Layne started heads-up play with a $701,000 to $80,000 chip lead over Johnny, and wrapped up his consecutive wins when he hit a set of tens on the river to defeat "The Oriental Express." Since that time, Layne has been known as "Back to Back Flack."

## ACTION HAND 69

### A Nine Nixes a Phenomenal Comeback

**T.J. Cloutier, Commentary**

When we started the final table at the 2000 WSOP championship event, Chris Ferguson had a lot of chips, the four others were close in chip count with $400,000 or more each, and I had $216,000. When I got up that morning, I formed a plan that I explained to my wife: "I'll let them knock each other out and try to get heads up with Chris." I thought that if my plan worked, I'd get to play heads-up with Chris, who figured to be in the lead because he had so many chips to start with.

Since I believe that poker is a game of mistakes, I wanted to let the others make the mistakes to put me in a position where I had a chance to win. They were all fine players, but none of them were experienced in final table play except Chris. That's why I thought that they would make major mistakes in crucial spots—and as it came up, that's exactly what happened. They dropped like flies. Finally, Chris and I were the only two left in action.

If I flopped a set and checked it to him, Chris would always catch some card that he thought was good enough to call with. When I had the best hand, I tried to let him pay, but not enough that it would make him drop his hand because I wanted to get paid on all those hands—that's what chipping away means. In other words, I tried to make the size of bet that I figured he would call. And he was getting nervous about it— you could see it in his eyes and mannerisms. His hands were shaking so badly that he pulled them behind his mountain of chips to conceal his tremors.

When we started playing heads up, Chris had $4,700,000 in chips and I had only $400,000—and I took the lead away from him. Never at any time did I get my money in with the worst hand. I kept chipping away at him, which means that I was trying to get Chris to take me off in spots. And he did.

By the time we got to the final hand, he had regained a slight lead over me. I could see that he was getting worried, and I thought there might be a chance that he was going to make a major error on a hand—and he did. Here's how our last hand came down:

When I looked down at A-Q, I shoved all my chips to the middle. Chris seemed to be caught by surprise. He took off his black Stetson, leaned back in his chair, and took a long time to decide what to do. Finally he called my all-in bet, the major mistake I'd been looking for. The crowd of spectators rose to its feet, and I could hear them gasp. We turned our cards face up and waited for the flop.

I stood up as the dealer slowly dealt the turn card, a useless king. Only one card left to go. If it was anything but a 9, I'd take down the pot and Chris would be so short on chips he could not have survived the blow. But luck is a part of poker.

The dealer turned over the 9♥ on the river that won the title for Chris.

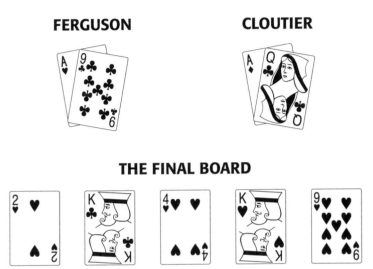

**FERGUSON**

**CLOUTIER**

**THE FINAL BOARD**

The way Chris explained things made sense to me—he said that he thought that on that one day, he couldn't beat me if we just played out the hands. He felt that he had to beat me in a major pot, so he decided to go with the hand. "I thought there was a very small chance that I had the best hand. And if I had the best hand, I was giving up a lot more by folding," he told the tournament reporter.

Obviously Chris thought that if he caught an ace, he'd have a hand, but he was in horrible position against my ace with a queen kicker. Actually it was his 9 kicker that made his hand a winner, not the ace.

And you know what? I saw that 9 coming before the dealer ever peeled it off. It was as though I was looking right through the deck. It had happened twice before heads-up when he had the lesser hand and drew out against me when the board paired on the end to tie our two hands.

The next day Tom drove me to the airport and we talked about the tournament and this hand. Next up is a recap of our conversation.

# AGONY AND ECSTASY AT THE FINAL TABLE:
## A CONVERSATION WITH T.J. CLOUTIER
### Tom McEvoy, Commentary

In one of the most dramatic finishes in the history of the World Series of Poker, Chris Ferguson was crowned the millennium's first World Champion of Poker. T.J. Cloutier came within a heartbeat of finally capturing the coveted title that he has come so close to winning three times in the past, coming up short by one river card. It was T.J.'s second runner-up finish; he also has finished third and fifth. It was a heartbreaker for T.J., who had clawed back from a 10-to-1 chip deficit heads-up and at one point had taken the lead over Chris.

After T.J. had made a fantastic comeback from such a big chip deficit to actually pull ahead, the action seesawed back and forth. The last pot was played all-in before the flop, with around $4.6 million of the $5.1 million chips in play, the largest single pot in WSOP history. The only thing that I've ever seen similar to that happened in 1982 when Dewey Tomko played Jack Straus heads-up for the championship. Dewey had the lead on the flop only to have it snatched from him at the river. With all the money in the middle, that hand settled the tournament. Similarly, with such a huge amount of money at stake and considering his other near misses, it truly was a torture for T.J. when his A-Q fell victim to Chris's A-9 on the river to give Chris the win.

Coming to the final table with the shortest stack, T.J.'s vast tournament experience helped him wade through the other four players at the final table. He successfully avoided major confrontations most of the time and when he did play a hand, he usually didn't get called. The one time that he was called, T.J. doubled through his adversary. He did the bob-and-weave until he got heads-up with Ferguson, at which time he opened up his game. Then he played a very controlled, aggressive game, coming over the top with reraises several times, causing Chris to lay down multiple hands. It was an excellent example of cat-and-mouse poker, with T.J.'s short stack being the cat and Chris's larger stack of chips being the mouse.

Looking at the long-haired, bearded Chris wearing sun glasses and a black felt hat with its brim curled low, I could almost feel his intensity. He looked determined, almost fierce, and the audience could see how badly he wanted to win. So did T.J. It is just unfortunate that one of them had to lose.

After coming back from such a chip deficit, losing at the end was all the more disappointing for T.J. When the fatal river card fell, T.J. took it like the man that he is, not even flinching. At the exact moment that the killer 9 hit the felt, I looked at T.J.'s face—he didn't show much emotion, which is one reason why he's always been considered one of the best tournament players that ever lived. But I knew that he was in pain. After such a truly bad beat, T.J. shook hands with Chris, congratulated him, and then began the inevitable interviews from the multitude of media covering the event.

The grand finale of the WSOP was a celebration of joy for Chris—who earlier had won the $5,000 seven-card stud title, making him the only double-bracelet winner in the 2000 WSOP— while at the same time I could feel T.J.'s heartbreak and torment. A total gentleman, Chris told me with complete sincerity, "I feel terrible for T.J.," because he knew how brutal losing like that could be.

Without a doubt, T.J. is the greatest player never to have won the "Big One." But as they said in Brooklyn all those years before the Dodgers moved to Los Angeles, "Just wait till next year." And actually, "next year" finally came once for the Brooklyn Dodgers—they won baseball's *World Series* in 1955 by beating the dreaded New York Yankees.

The day after the WSOP ended, I drove T.J. to McCarran airport to catch a plane to Dallas—he was going home at last (about $900,00 richer, I might add). Along the way, I became so engrossed in our conversation about the play at the final table that T.J. had to gave me several tips—not about poker but how to get to the airport!

**How are you feeling after your near miss in the championship event?**

I'm feeling fine—how can you squawk at winning $896,000?! I thought that I played well, in fact as good as I've ever played in my life. After coming back from almost nothing, I got my chips in there three different times and each time I had Chris in situations where he had to outdraw me. You can't do any better than that. The first time, he had to pair the board to tie me; the second time, he had to match my high card on the board to tie; and the third time he had to catch a 9 down the river with three outs for all the money. When we started playing heads-up he had $4,700,00 and I had $400,000. I chopped my way back to where I was equal with him, so I can't fault my play. Lady Luck came into the picture this time, that's all.

**You certainly gave a classic performance on how to play a short stack.**

Every time I got my money in, I got it in with the best hand. *Get on the freeway here, Tom.*

**That's all that anybody can do. It was cruel to lose to a three-outer like that.**

You just have to get a little lucky. (Now get in the left lane, okay?) All you can do is play your best and hope for a few breaks here and there. Of course, I had a game plan going into the final table. My plan was to let Chris destroy the other ones, or let them destroy themselves, and then try to take him off. I wanted to get to at least second place, but I knew that I was short-chipped and so for the time being, I stayed out of Chris's road. I worked on Hassan in one hand and that was all. Chris broke all the rest of them, and that was perfect. Every now and then, a game plan works.

**Your tournament experience helped you wade through the other four finalists. It seems to me that the player with the biggest disappointment at the Series might have been newcomer Jeff Shulman, who went from the chip lead seven-handed to out of the tournament in about 20 minutes.**

I was playing at Shulman's table. He was very aggressive, but he also became just a little bit "chip happy," I think. Ferguson moved all his chips in with a pair of sixes and Shulman called him with a pair of sevens. He had the best hand, don't misunderstand me, but with his chip lead he didn't need to make this play—he didn't need to be involved in the pot at all. At the time, the handwriting was on the wall: Shulman had $1.5 million and doubled Ferguson up when a 6 flopped. Ferguson got lucky, sure, but there was no reason in the world for Shulman to have played a big pot in that spot with two sevens. *Turn right here, Tom.*

**That was a key hand seven-handed and a more experienced player probably would have passed it. The other key hand happened when you, Chris and Jeff were involved in a three-way pot later in the action.**

Yes. In the last pot of the night, the blinds were $15,000/$30,000 and Chris brought it in for $90,000. I raised it to $390,000 with pocket jacks—I didn't want anybody with a lone ace calling me. Jeff, who was sitting behind me with pocket kings, moved all-in. Then Chris also moved all-in. I knew that my two jacks were toilet paper, so I threw them away. One of them was going to get broke on the hand and I was going to get to the final table. Chris had pocket aces and they stood up against Jeff's pocket kings.

**A pair of kings is a hard hand to get away from. Of course, Chris wouldn't have been in the position to break him if Jeff hadn't already been in that previous hand with two sevens. Had he made any other plays that you questioned?**

No, he played aggressively, raising with a lot of ace-type hands like A-10 or A-6 from around back all the time. At an earlier table, I had played back at Jeff a couple of times. One time he thought that I might be on a stone bluff and took about five minutes to think it through. He was considering coming back over the top of me with his A-K, but instead he mucked the hand. I had two kings in the hole, which I showed to him. "Boy, I had a real bad read on you there," he said. *Go straight here, okay, Tom?*

**Looks like he did the right thing "by accident." But getting back to the final table action, there was no doubt in anyone's mind that if you had won that last hand, Chris would have**

**been in a lot of trouble. At the end, Chris mentioned how well you played.**

Chris was very gracious to me. I thought that overall I played well in the tournament and so did he. Heads-up with me, Chris kept putting himself in situations where he had to call big bets with weak hands. I wasn't willing to put myself in that type of situation.

**I thought Chris might've been a little bit intimidated by you, and he suddenly quit catching cards for a while.**

Twice he caught A-K or aces, but both times I threw my hand away so that he didn't get any play on them. One time I had A♦ Q♦ and flat called. Things like that kept him from knowing exactly where I was coming from, which was my whole idea with those plays. In that particular hand, the flop came 6-4-2 with two diamonds. He bet about $60,000 and I just called with two overcards and the nut flush draw. A queen came at the river and I bet. He called. I showed him the queen and won the pot. I had read the hand correctly. I took a small lead and then it seesawed back and forth a bit. At the end I had $2.3 million to his $2.8 million. If I had won the last hand, he would've had only $500,000 left. *Get in the left lane for departing flights, Tom.*

**Your coming from so far back to take second made this one of the most dramatic final tables I've ever seen. The 9 that hit for Chris was a $600,000 river card plus the world championship. But I was surprised that he called your all-in raise with only an A-9.**

Chris himself said that he thought that I was outplaying him at that point and that his only chance of beating me was to gamble and hope to get lucky. I don't fault him on that. If it had been meant to be, I would have won it. But I'll stack my record up against all of them—four final-table finishes with a second and a third in the last three years.

**You and Doyle Brunson are the only players who have placed in the top five four times. Stu Ungar won three times and was ninth one other time. Brunson had two firsts, a second and a third.**

And I plan to make it again next year or however long it takes.

**We're almost at the airport terminal, T.J., so I just want you to know that I think you handled defeat like a gentleman.**

How could I have handled it any differently? I felt that if I went down, it would be on the last card. Maybe next time that river card will belong to me. *How did we get to Terminal Two, Tom? We want Terminal One, don't we?*

**Ooops!**

PART THREE

# LIMIT HOLD'EM HANDS INTRODUCTION

## TOM MCEVOY

In this part, you'll learn the best way to play various types of hands in limit hold'em freeze-out tournaments with structures similar to major, big buy-in events. Most of the action hands we depict are unsuited because we want you to realize that the ranks of the cards you play are more important than whether they are suited. Some players use being suited as the reason to play certain hands when they should be looking more at their high-card value.

If poker were purely a game of skill, the best players would win all the time, but we all know that doesn't happen. Luck plays a greater role in tournaments than in side games because of the escalating limits and the rarity of getting premium starting hands in a compressed amount of time. The slower the limits go up, the more important tournament skills become. The faster the limits go up, the more significant the luck factor.

In tournaments with world-class fields of contestants whose skills are fairly equal, the player who catches the best cards that particular day and plays them well over time is the person most likely to win the tournament. Therefore, because so many world-class players enter the major tournaments, no one has a huge edge over anyone else.

Players with lesser skills sometimes win tournaments or finish high in the money, and it happens often enough to keep them in the chase. Even in World Series of Poker events, I occasionally have seen mediocre players make it to the final table—but I have never seen an even remotely weak player win it all, no matter how lucky he was. And it doesn't happen often enough to discourage better players, because they know that skill will dominate luck in the long run.

There is no magic formula for longevity in a tournament. All of the major tournament players that I have talked with about what happens when you get to that $150/$300 round or the $200/$400 round agree that you just have to catch hands at those betting levels. You can't manufacture a hand that doesn't exist. What you must do instead is play a patient, controlled game and give yourself a chance to get lucky. If you play too recklessly on marginal hands and get knocked out early, you can't make it to the higher levels where, if your hands hold up, you have a good chance of winning.

Luck is always a factor in tournaments, but your tournament skills are far more important in maximizing your chances of winning. You must have skill to survive long enough to get lucky. The more correct decisions you make in the earlier rounds, the better your chances of surviving to the later rounds and getting a good rush of cards. Knowing how to make the most of the rush is what separates the very best players from the rest.

In *Championship107 Tournament Hold'em Hands*, T.J. and I do our best to help you sharpen your skills in playing limit and no-limit hold'em, so that when the right cards start coming your way, you'll be there to catch them like lightning in a bottle.

# WINNING WITH ACES

When you're playing a tournament and look down at the boss hand, two aces, you're on top of the world. You've been waiting for this great hand and now it's yours. You want to win a big pot with your aces, but that's not always the result you get. A lot of times, it depends on your skill in tricky situations.

Let's start out with this basic premise: It doesn't matter what stage of the tournament you're in or what your stack size is, always bring the pot in for a raise before the flop with pocket aces. Whether you're in first, middle, or last position, raise with A-A. Don't give any free flops. Never limp with two aces unless there is a maniac sitting behind you who raises every pot. In that case, since you know that he's going to raise the pot anyway, you might limp in and then put in the third bet after he raises.

The flop is where you make your most important decision about how to play pocket aces. Let's look at some good flops and some bad ones, and see how you might play A-A to make the most profit.

## ACTION HAND 70
### Playing Aces in Early Position

Some players seem to think that slow-playing aces is a good idea. But suppose you have A♥ A♠ in first position and just limp into the pot. Then what happens? Five other players also limp in, making it a six-way pot. The flop comes:

### YOUR HAND

### FLOP

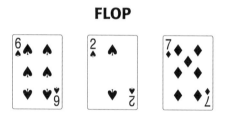

There's a pretty fair chance that someone has two pair, sevens and sixes, since a lot of limit players like to play middle connectors. On this flop, an opponent also could have a set, an open-ended straight draw, or a flush draw. If you had raised with your aces, you probably would have narrowed the field enough that you would only have had to beat one or two players and, if the flop came with raggedy cards, there would be a pretty good chance that you had the best hand.

The idea is to limit the field when you've been dealt two aces. You don't mind playing aces against one or two players, but you don't want to have to play against a lot of opponents.

A pair of aces is the best hand that you can start with in limit hold'em, and you might as well try to win a pot without giving your opponents every reason to beat you. If the players who called your bet or raise before the flop are all regular players, lead at it on the flop unless big connected cards hit the board.

## ACTION HAND 71

### Playing A-A on a Flop with Three Big Connectors

Any three big connected cards is a dangerous flop to your pair of aces: K-Q-J, K-Q-10, K-J-10, or Q-J-10. Say that you raise from a front position before the flop with A♦ A♣ and an opponent reraises. You reraise and he calls, so you see the flop heads-up:

### YOUR HAND

### FLOP

If you have put in at least three bets before the flop, you had better shut down. Don't lead at the pot because there is the possibility that a set, two pair, or a straight is out against you. When you're playing in a tournament, why risk losing a ton of irreplaceable chips with your aces? If somebody comes out betting at you, make up your mind right then whether you should play any further with your aces or throw them away.

Now suppose you raised before the flop with your pocket rockets, two players called, and the flop comes:

### YOUR HAND

### FLOP

In this case, you probably should lead with your aces. Although a K-10 or 10-8 would give somebody a straight, players usually won't raise or call a raise with those types of hands. Of course, somebody could have flopped two pair, such as queens and jacks, or even a set, but you can't be overly afraid of that possibility.

## ACTION HAND 72

### When the Flop Comes with a Pair

If a pair is on board, especially a high pair, use caution in playing pocket aces. Someone may have made trips—especially if you did not raise preflop. Players like to come into unraised pots with hands such as K-Q, Q-J, Q-10, and J-10, especially from mid to late positions. Suppose you "forgot" to raise before the flop, and two opponents limped behind you. The flop comes:

**YOUR HAND**

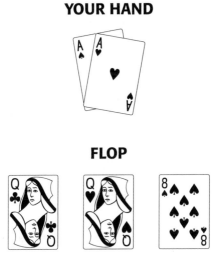

**FLOP**

You bet on the flop, one opponent calls, and the second one raises. Now what do you do? When there is a pair on board and you get raised, slow down and reevaluate the situation before proceeding. There's a good chance you've been outflopped. You might flat call the raise to see the turn card, and then make your decision as to how to proceed.

## *ACTION HAND 73*

### When You Flop a Four Flush

Now suppose the board comes with three cards of the same suit and you have the ace in that suit. What do you do?

### YOUR HAND

### FLOP

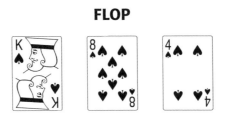

This is another time when you should lead with your aces. Even if somebody has flopped a flush, you have a redraw to the nut flush. See how the hand gets played out. If you lead and it gets raised and reraised, you know that somebody probably already has a flush. In limit hold'em, you probably would continue with the hand to see at least one more card.

## *ACTION HAND 74*

### Playing A-A on a Rainbow Flop

Suppose you're holding pocket aces in a front position and you raise before the flop. Two opponents flat call the raise, so you're in a three-way pot. The flop comes:

## YOUR HAND

## FLOP

You can't give your opponents credit for flopping two pair or a set—there aren't that many two-pair hands or sets flopped in poker. Although I've seen limit players come in with hands like J-7 suited or pocket deuces, they are less like to do that if a player in early position has raised preflop. You have to be very aggressive, so lead at the pot.

## ACTION HAND 75

### When You Flop an Ace

Of course, your ideal flop has an ace in it.

**YOUR HAND**

**FLOP**

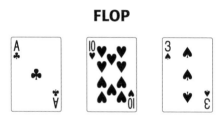

When you flop an ace, just keep leading at the pot. Why would you miss a bet? Now, suppose that no ace comes on the flop. You bet, an opponent calls, and an ace comes on the turn.

**YOUR HAND**

## TURN

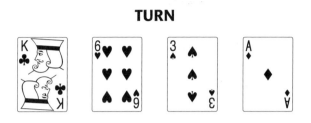

Should you go ahead and bet, or should you check in the hope that your opponent will bet and give you a chance to check-raise him? You should bet. Don't try to set a trap by checking to him. If you check, he usually will check as well. Then when you bet on the end, he may throw his hand away and you've lost one or two bets.

In summary, forget about limping with aces in the first two seats. I've seen lots of players lose big pots because they limped with big pairs from up front and let somebody get into the pot with a 9-8 or 6-5. Then their opponent flops two pair or a straight and those aces are history. Don't give free cards!

# PLAYING ACES IN LATE POSITION

Suppose you have a pair of aces in a late position. The people at your table are playing pretty decent poker, and somebody brings it in for a raise and another player reraises it. Should you reraise? Yes—put in the third raise. Don't think about trying to trap by just flat calling, because sometimes when you try to trap, you don't get full value out of the hand. So put in the third raise and hope that you get called by both of your opponents. You want to have the strength position. Remember that before the flop there's no such thing as the nuts, so if you get unlucky and lose the pot, so be it.

## *ACTION HAND 76*

### Playing Aces in Late Position

Three players have limped into the pot. Holding A-A in the cutoff seat, you raise. The button and the small blind fold. The big blind and all three of the limpers call, so five of you see the flop.

The flop comes:

### YOUR HAND

### FLOP

One of your opponents leads at the pot. You think he's probably leading at you with A-K. When he bets, raise him so that any of the little straggling hands that might have come into the pot will get out. You want to get it heads-up if you can. If he bets at you again on fourth street, just call; if he checks, bet. If the board rags off or pairs a little card on fifth street, raise if he bets into you.

But what if a straight card or a flush card comes on the river? Look at this final board:

## YOUR HAND

## THE FINAL BOARD

    With three flush cards on board, you usually call a single bet—unless you know that your opponent would virtually never bet anything except a straight or a flush in this situation. If the action is checked to you, what's your best play? You should generally check against tricky opponents and bet against timid or predictable players who don't usually check strong hands.

# WINNING WITH KINGS

Playing two kings in limit hold'em is pretty cut and dried—play them the same way you treat aces. But you have to be ready to shut down if an ace hits the board on the flop.

If an opponent in an early position raises the pot before the flop and another player calls the raise in front of you, reraise with your two kings. You'd hate for one of them to have an A-4 and then see an ace hit on the flop. Make them pay to get a chance at catching that kind of flop with their weak ace. Of course, there are some weak limit hold'em players who wouldn't lay down an ace-anything hand before the flop for all the tea in China. But even though you might lose to them now and then, these are the kinds of players that you want to play against.

You have to play it by feel. You must raise with kings preflop and if someone raises in front of you, reraise. You want to get it heads-up. If you put in raise number two and your opponent puts in raise number three, you have to call him. There's a chance that you'll be up against aces, but not necessarily. Again, it gets down to watching your opponents. How aggressively do they play two jacks or small pairs? Do they put in a third bet with two queens? Always be alert.

In summary, play two kings very aggressively before the flop and hope that an ace doesn't hit the board. Remember that when you're playing against only one or two players, a big pair has a good chance of holding up, but if you're playing against a big field in the hand, and all you have is one pair, you can't be nearly as aggressive. This is why you always raise before the flop with K-K to try to get it heads-up.

# WHEN AN ACE HITS ON THE FLOP

If an ace comes out on the flop, ask yourself whether there are players at your table who will bet an underpair if an ace hits the board. If you check, will they bet with two jacks or two tens? Although this sometimes happens, they usually will have an ace if the pot has been raised before the flop. Know the people you're playing against and remember how they have been playing their hands.

## *ACTION HAND 77*

### Playing Kings on an Ace-High Flop

Suppose you have K♥ K♠ in a four-way pot. The flop comes:

### YOUR HAND

## FLOP

The first person to act comes out betting and the next player just calls. The action is up to you with one player left to act behind you. What do you do? Your kings aren't looking quite as good as they did before the flop, are they? In fact, they're looking a whole lot like losers! So you throw them in the muck.

---

**KEY CONCEPT**

Don't be afraid to fold pocket kings if an ace hits the board and an opponent bets into you or raises.

---

Never be afraid to throw away two kings if an ace hits the board and someone bets into you or raises. You're a big dog to the hand, so you have to get away from it. After the flop, you have two outs twice, two more kings to hit on fourth street and fifth street. With an ace on board, what do you have?

After the flop you have to play the kings as the board dictates. You face the same types of danger flops with pocket kings that you face with pocket aces, only more so because of the danger of an ace flopping. You're starting with the second-best hand that you can be dealt, but when you have kings, it seems like every card left in the deck is an ace!

## *ACTION HAND 78*

### When You Flop a Flush Draw

Suppose you have the K♥ K♠ and three spades come out on the flop:

### YOUR HAND

### FLOP

Should you continue with the flush draw? Yes. You have second pair to the A♠, and your kings beat the board's second-highest card, the 10♠. You could make the nut flush if another spade comes, or three kings if a kings comes. Play this hand through the turn, unless the board pairs. Then you have to make a decision as to whether your draw is still alive. In a big action pot, a pair on the board can mean that a full house is out against you.

On the river, you have to make a judgment call as to what you should do if you miss your flush and a player bets into you. Try to get inside your opponent's head. Would he bet with a pair lower than aces or a lower flush draw than yours? If you think he would, call the bet. But if you think he has what he is representing—a flush or an ace—fold.

What if you're not heads-up at the river? Suppose you have two opponents. The first player bets into you and you still have an opponent yet to act behind you. In that case, you should usually fold; you don't want to risk being raised by the player behind you. Getting put in the middle is not a happy place.

# WINNING WITH QUEENS AND JACKS

In limit hold'em, pocket queens is a raising hand before the flop from any position—but is it a reraising hand? Sometimes, but not always. Remember that there are two overcards to the queen—ace and king—that people play all the time in limit hold'em. Suppose a solid player in seat one raises before the flop and another solid player calls the raise before it gets to you. One or the other of them might have two aces, two kings, or A-K. Do you just call with pocket queens, or do you reraise. You just call, you don't reraise.

Now suppose an opponent in the first seat has raised and a solid player in the second seat has reraised. You're in the third seat with a bunch of players to act behind you. What do you do now? Unless you're playing against maniacs, you throw your queens away. Although you've picked up a pretty nice hand, you don't have any money involved in the pot, and since it's been raised and reraised before you've even had a chance to act, it's easy to just throw them away in this spot. So what if the player in the first seat only has two tens? The player next to him might have two aces, two kings, A-K, or even A-Q.

## ACTION HAND 79

### Playing Queens in the Big Blind

Let's say that you have pocket queens in the big blind. The pot has been raised and reraised and now it's up to you. You've already got one bet in the pot, so you call. The flop comes:

**YOUR HAND**

**FLOP**

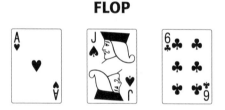

Now what do you do? You're the first to bet, so you check. The raiser bets and the reraiser calls. Any time an ace or king comes on the flop, you're through with this hand. You fold.

Of course, if a queen comes, you're in Fat City. Take a look at this flop:

**YOUR HAND**

## FLOP

If a queen flops along with an ace or king, play it strong. Bet on the flop. Sets don't flop all that often, so don't be too afraid of someone having three kings. Against this type of flop, your opponents might put you on a king when you bet, and if one of them has an A-K, he's probably going to raise you. In that case don't reraise, just smooth-call the raise and then play for a check-raise on the turn.

Now suppose once again that you are in the big blind with pocket queens and a player in late position raises with no more than two limpers already in the pot. In this case, reraising with your queens definitely is in order to try to narrow the field and get it heads-up if possible.

## *ACTION HAND 80*

### Playing an Open-Ended Straight Draw or Overpair on the Flop

Suppose you have raised the pot before the flop with Q♣ Q♥. The flop comes:

### YOUR HAND

### FLOP

This is a good flop for your hand because it gives you an overpair and an open-ended straight draw. Just hope you're not up against a K-Q! Of course, this would be a much better flop for you:

### YOUR HAND

## FLOP

In this scenario you hope that your opponent has something like an A-J so that you can make a play with the queens.

Players often tell me how they keep getting two queens beat, but remember that Q-Q is still a very good hand. It's just that as you descend the ladder on the ranks of the pairs, you have to be more and more careful because the lower you go, the more overcards there are to contend with. Kings have aces as overcards, queens have aces and kings—and in a raised pot some of these cards are almost sure to be out. So, if the pot has been raised and reraised, there's a pretty good chance that even though you might have the best starting hand, somebody has one or two overcards ready to beat your queens.

Some players raise with middle pairs of 7 or higher. Say that an opponent raises with A-K, you call with two queens, and a player with 7-7 also calls. He has two sevens to catch and the other player can land an ace or a king to beat you. But bear in mind that although you're less of a mathematical favorite versus two opponents, you're still the money favorite.

> **KEY CONCEPT**
> Good players get away from bad situations.

Remember that if you're playing in a cash game you can play a lot more aggressively with two queens than in a tournament. In tournaments, you sometimes simply have to get away from a hand. The good players get away from bad situations—they're not afraid to throw a hand away. Sometimes you even throw away a winner, but if you can't throw away a winner once in a while, you can't win at poker, because then you're just a calling station. I've never felt bad about throwing away a winner when I wasn't heavily involved in a pot. When I throw a hand away it is because I believe that the percentages are in *their* favor, not mine. The hand hasn't cost me that much—why should I give it a chance to cost me a ton of chips and find myself suddenly down to a short stack?

## ACTION HAND 81

### When You Flop a Four Flush

Suppose you have the Q♣ Q♥ in late position. You raise preflop and two opponents call. The flop comes 10♣ 7♣ 2♣.

You have an overpair and a four flush. From there onward, you're playing draw poker. If someone bets into you, you don't necessarily want to make the flush because he might already have a made flush or the A♣ or K♣ for a draw to the flush. There's still a pretty good chance that you have the best hand on the flop, however, so you can bet the flop if you're first to act, or call a bet if someone bets into you.

Suppose another club comes on the turn.

### YOUR HAND

## TURN

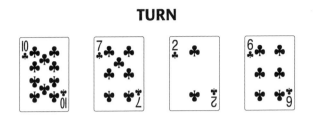

How do your play your hand? It depends on several factors. How many players are in the pot? Was the pot raised before the flop? If so, a suited ace or king are cards that someone definitely might be holding. If you're playing heads-up, remember that your opponent called on the flop. How well do you know this player? Is he the type who bets or calls with a drawing hand? You need to use the best tactic, one that won't cause you to lose a lot of money in this pot. If you're first to act, check to find out what your opponent does, or check-call if he bets.

This is a situation where your poker playing ability comes into play. There is no one way to play this pot, so you have to be ready to go with your instincts and make your best decision on the turn.

Now suppose a blank comes on the turn, but a club comes on the river.

## YOUR HAND

## THE FINAL BOARD

Let's assume that you're playing heads-up. Check if you're first to act and then just call if your opponent bets behind you. You don't want to risk any more than you have to if he has the A♣ or K♣. Of course, he also might have a lower flush or even a straight if he came into the pot with 8♣ 5♥, for example, though that is unlikely. If your opponent is first to act and bets into you, just call. You don't want to risk getting reraised and losing two or three bets to this hand.

## ACTION HAND 82

### When You Flop Top Set on a Dangerous Board

Here's a perfect example of a dangerous board. You make top set on the flop, but there's also a straight possibility out there.

## YOUR HAND

## FLOP

What do you do? You still lead with your trip queens if you are first to act. If you get raised, call the raise, but you should stop leading at the pot unless the board pairs. What if a player bets in front of you on the flop? Raise him. But what if he reraises your raise? In that case, you have two options.

### Action Choice One

You can just call and hope the board pairs. Unless one of your opponents raised before the flop, there is the distinct possibility that an A-K is not in play.

### Action Choice Two

You can reraise, which is exactly what I would do. If the guy has A-K, more power to him—but you still have redraws to the boss hand.

I don't suggest *not* betting the hand or *not* raising with it—why give your opponents a free card? If you're just checking along and giving free cards, an opponent with a king, 9, or 8 could catch a middle-buster straight and beat you. For example, if a 9 comes on the turn, there are four cards to a straight on board and suddenly your set doesn't look too good with only one card to come. So, you have to lead with your queens—you can't allow everybody to get into the deck against you without having to pay for the privilege.

# HOW TO PLAY JACKS

You can raise with pocket jacks from any position when you are the first player in the pot. If you get reraised, just call—after you see the flop, you can decide whether to continue with the hand. Now suppose you're in late position and a couple of players have limped in front of you—you're still going to raise the pot, because you want to eliminate the blinds and everyone still to act behind you, if possible, and to build the pot. The number of players who are in the hand determines the value of your jacks. The more players in the pot, even if an overcard does not flop, the more vulnerable you are. Heads-up, two jacks is a big-big hand.

If you're in the cutoff seat or on the button, you should raise with the jacks if the pot hasn't been raised yet. Your raise might knock out the people between you and the first bettor. If someone reraises, just smooth-call—if you get unlucky and an ace, king, or queen flops, you can always get rid of the hand at the minimum cost.

Obviously if the flop comes jack-high, or if it has any jack in it, that's a big-big flop for you. But when it comes with overcards and you have two or more opponents, there's a pretty good chance that you're already beaten—and you're down to four outs, two outs twice.

### ACTION HAND 83

## When You Flop an Open-Ended Straight Draw or Overpair

Suppose you flop an overpair and an open-ended straight draw.

### YOUR HAND

### FLOP

This is not a bad flop to your hand but it isn't one that you can take to the bank either. Remember once again that limit hold'em is all about big cards—people call raises with Q-J in this game and if someone is in there with a Q-J, you're trying to catch a queen for a tie. As you get lower on the totem pole with your pair, other hands seem to be bigger in limit play (A-K, A-Q, even K-Q is only an 11 to 10 dog against two jacks). Two jacks just don't cut the mustard that well—you'll want to play against only one opponent and hope that you get a small flop or a jack.

---

**KEY CONCEPT**

Limit Hold'em is a game of big cards.

---

## *ACTION HAND 84*

### Playing Jacks on a Broken Board

Now look at this flop when you hold pocket jacks:

### YOUR HAND

### FLOP

A broken board is a good flop for your jacks. Certainly someone could have a pocket pair to match the flop, but that could happen with any hand. In that case, the way your opponents play will dictate what you do with the jacks. You'll definitely bet if it's checked to you, and if somebody bets in front of you, you might even put in one raise.

Raising on the flop in this scenario is a lot better than waiting until fourth street because, in many cases, you can limit the field, which protects your overpair from draw-outs.

For example, suppose a 10 comes on the turn, giving no straight or flush possibilities on the board.

### YOUR HAND

### TURN

Somebody might have made two pair, tens and nines—players like to play the connectors in hold'em. Or an opponent holding cards such as Q-J could have picked up a straight draw, but that's good for you. You like your opponents to pick up a draw with one card to come—if they get there, so be it, but you're still a big favorite in the hand.

## Playing J-J Late in the Tournament

Late in a tournament the jacks are no better or worse than they are early on if you're playing at a full table. The limits are higher but the hand values remain the same any time the table is full. A pair of jacks is a lot better hand short-handed than it is in a full ring because you can be aggressive with them before the flop. For example, if you're at the final table with five players left, you can play pocket jacks a lot stronger than you could when the final table started with nine or ten players. Just remember that if an ace, king, or queen hits the flop, your hand may be worth nothing.

# WINNING WITH ACE-KING

Big Slick is what everybody in the rest of the world calls A-K, but in Texas we call it "Walking Back to Houston." In the old days, we used to say that if you went to Dallas and played A-K enough times in no-limit hold'em, you'd get broke and have start walking all the way back home to Houston.

To be successful in tournaments, you have to win *with* an A-K and you have to win when you're playing *against* an A-K. In other words, you have to win the 11 to 10 situations.

In limit hold'em A-K is a big hand, a reraising hand, whether it's suited or not. Being suited just means it's a little more valuable, that's all. There's an old story about two guys who both held an A-K. The first one says, "Well, I have A♣ K♣ and you have A♥ K♠. I only need three cards in my suit to make a flush."

"Well, hell!" the second man answers. "I only need four cards in two suits—I have *two* flush draws against your one!"

In any position other than the small or big blind, you can reraise with A-K. And if you've been watching your opponents, you might even *reraise* against most of them. You can raise from the blinds but don't make a habit of reraising, because you will have to act first from the flop on, which puts you out of position. Always remember that A-K is a *positional* hand.

---

**KEY CONCEPT**

You must win the 11 to 10 coin tosses in tournaments. You have to win **with** A-K and you have to win **against** A-K.

---

If you're around back and somebody has raised in front of you, reraise with A-K because you have them on the defensive, and they will have to act first after the flop. If you're in the first three positions, bring it in for a raise. If you're in middle position, reraise with A-K. And again, if you're in the small or big blind, the most you should do is raise with the hand—do not reraise with it.

## *ACTION HAND 85*

### When You Flop Two Overcards

Suppose you're in the small blind with the A♠ K♥. Several players are in the pot and the flop comes something like:

### YOUR HAND

## FLOP

You don't have a pair, so you should check. A lot of people like to lead into the field with the A-K against this type of flop. Then they get played with, and almost invariably call the raise. Here's a typical scenario: Joe Blow bets it, somebody raises him, and he calls the raise because he has two big overcards. A rag comes on fourth street and Joe still doesn't have anything. He can't lead at it again but he calls when somebody else puts in a fourth-street bet—he's trying to catch that ace or king on fifth street because he has sucked out on the river several times before. But the percentages are way against him.

Most of today's limit hold'em players play A-K—or ace-anything, really—like it's the Holy Grail. They raise with A-Q, A-J, A-10, and even A-9 and worse. A lot of players love playing any suited ace, and they like to raise with those hands too. You're a big favorite over these types of hands with an A-K and that's why you always reraise with it *in position* (when you don't have to act first after the flop). Of course, you also lose a lot of those pots when your opponents spike their only outs, but in the long run you're going to win a lot more than you lose because you started with the best hand.

I was sweating T.J. during a limit hold'em tournament when an interesting situation came up. With limits at $2,000/$4,000, the first player raised, the next player reraised, and the guy in fifth position called. T.J. was in the big blind with A-K in the hole. What do you think he did? He threw it away!

At least 80 percent of the time you should fold an A-K in this type of situation. All you have invested in the pot is your blind. It's going to cost you a double raise to see the flop when you might already be up against aces, kings, or even a suited A-K, which also would be a favorite over your hand. Furthermore, you're out of position on the hand.

## ACTION HAND 86

### Playing A-K on a Dangerous Flop

If you don't hit a pair to your A-K, any flop is dangerous! For example, suppose you raised with the A♠ K♥ before the flop and two opponents called. The board comes:

### YOUR HAND

### FLOP

What do you do with Big Slick? Are you going to play it in the hope of catching a 10, ace, or king? A lot of players do, but we don't suggest it. Other than catching a 10, nothing else will make your hand the nuts. If you catch an ace or king, it could make a straight or two pair for somebody else. Of course, you might be up against a weak queen such as Q-7 suited—people play some strange hands in limit hold'em—and if you catch an ace or king on the turn, it would make you're A-K the boss hand. But for every time that you catch the perfect card, you'll miss it seven or eight times. Do you think you could ever make enough money in the one pot where you catch to make up what you lost in all the other pots?

## ACTION HAND 87

### Trapping with A-K

In a tournament, the only time you should try to trap is when you have the nuts, when you cannot be outdrawn. Say that you have the A♠ K♥ in a later position than your sole opponent. The flop comes Q♥ J♦ 10♠.

Your opponent bets and you just flat call because you've decided to trap him. Then the board pairs on the turn.

### YOUR HAND

### TURN

Your opponent bets into you again. What do you do now? You have to decide how you want to play the hand. Are you going to raise him? Yes, give him one shot. If he just calls your raise, there are several possibilities as to what he could be holding. He could also have A-K, he could've made a full house, or he might have K♦ 9♦ for a lesser straight and a gutshot flush draw. But if he comes back over the top of you with a reraise, all you have is a crying call at best if you know that he's a good player.

# WINNING WITH BIG CONNECTORS

In addition to A-K, you can play several other hands with big connectors in limit hold'em tournaments. Although hands such as A-Q, A-J, K-Q and Q-J are not as powerful as Big Slick, they can be profitable in the right situations. Let's start off by discussing A-Q, the second-best connected hand in hold'em.

## HOW TO PLAY A-Q

An A-Q is a good hand in limit hold'em because so many people these days play lesser holdings, such as small connectors and any ace. If the flop comes ace-high or queen-high, you have a pretty good hand. When the flop comes queen high, you have top pair-top kicker; and when it comes ace-high you have top pair with second-best kicker. You usually would prefer the queen to hit the flop rather than the ace—except, of course, when your opponent has pocket kings. You would like to be up against a K-Q or Q-J when the flop comes queen-high because then you're sitting in clover.

You can raise with A-Q from any position to limit the field, just as with A-K, but you don't usually want to reraise with it. There are a few situations in a tournament, however, when you might even reraise with A-Q. Suppose you're sitting on the button and a player raises the pot with only enough chips to make one more bet. In that case, you're going to reraise to put him all in. By raising him all-in, you're not going to get blown out on the flop if it doesn't come with anything that helps you—and hopefully, you will knock him out. The reraise usually will take the blinds out as well.

Another situation where you can reraise with A-Q is when you're in very late position and an aggressive player sitting to your immediate right raises. You could reraise in this spot because you probably have the best hand, and you also have position on him.

## ACTION HAND 88

### Playing A-Q on an Ace-High Flop

You're the button with Ah Qc. Everyone limps around to the aggressive player in the cutoff seat, who fires in a raise. You reraise, the blinds fold, and the cutoff just calls your reraise. The flop comes:

### YOUR HAND

### FLOP

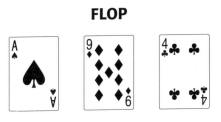

Oops! Suppose you're up against an A-K—now you're trapped. Although A-Q is a very good hand in limit hold'em, you still don't want to put yourself in a bind with it. If your aggressive opponent comes out firing on this flop, play it slow and just call.

## ACTION HAND 89

### Playing A-Q on a Coordinated Flop

Suppose you have the A♥ Q♣ and the flop comes:

### YOUR HAND

### FLOP

Although a lot of people play K-Q in limit hold'em, don't automatically put an opponent on it. You can continue with the hand to see the turn. If a king comes, you will have the stone nuts (A-K-Q-J-10), and an 8 will give you the second-best possible straight (Q-J-10-9-8).

# HOW TO PLAY A-J

An A-J is big trouble in most limit hold'em tournament situations. You play it somewhat similarly to a K-Q, the next hand we discuss in this section. An A-J is a little more attractive if it's suited, of course, but too many players overrate the value of suited cards. This is a hand that a lot of people play from almost any position—but if they play it from an early spot, they're making a mistake. You must have the right set of conditions to play an A-J. If you are the first player to act in a full ring with aggressive players sitting behind you, this hand is a loser.

Remember that in tournaments, players usually play a little more solid than they do in cash games. This means that if anybody comes into the pot in front of you, or if it gets raised behind you, you probably are already beaten. Also, you probably are beat if someone brings it in for a raise in front of you, especially if a player sitting in the first two or three positions put in the raise. Or suppose you come in first and decide to bring it in for a raise and someone raises behind you—you probably are up against a better starting hand that has position on you. The time when you like to play A-J is when you are in middle to late position and are the first to act.

There are times, however, when you might play an A-J very strongly. For example, if you are short-stacked, you may commit to the hand, particularly if an action player raises from late position and you know that he has been bullying the table with a big stack of chips. If that is the case, you may reraise with A-J to get more money in before the flop with the intention of committing the rest of your stack after the flop.

You also might defend the big blind with A-J against a late position raiser. However if a solid player raises from very first position when you are in one of the blinds, you don't like this hand at all. What is he raising with? And what are you trying to make with this hand? The ideal flop is K-Q-10, but the chances of getting that flop are remote.

## ACTION HAND 90

### Playing A-J on an Ace-High Flop

Suppose you're in the big blind with the A♣ J♦. An opponent in middle position raised preflop. Everybody folds around to you. Since you've never seen him raise with any hand other than a big pair, you put him on pocket kings, queens or jacks. The flop comes:

**YOU**             **OPPONENT**

**FLOP**

If your opponent indeed has a big pair (other than aces), he probably cannot give you any further action with the ace on the board. If you follow your instinct and lead into him from the big blind, he probably will give up the hand, so you can't win any extra bets with the hand.

But suppose you're wrong about the nature of his hand. Take a look at this flop:

**YOU**             **OPPONENT**

## FLOP

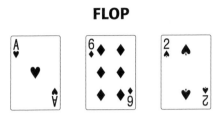

In this scenario, since he has a bigger ace than your A-J, you're in trouble with a mediocre kicker. If he has raised with A-K or A-Q, you're going to get all the action you want and more. The only problem is that you're down to a three-out hand to hit your kicker, so you're in bad shape. These are the kinds of situations that we urge you to avoid as often as possible. This often means passing the hand or at least playing it very selectively.

Late in the tournament when you are nearing the payoff spots, A-J is a reasonably good hand to be aggressive with. It becomes more valuable to you, even in a full ring, because so many players are just trying to survive to come in the money. However, if there are a lot of big stacks at your table willing to mix it up, that's *not* the time for you to become aggressive with A-J. Of course, if you are the one with the big stack against a lot of short ones, A-J is a good gambling hand in the very late stage of the tournament.

You have to use good judgment in playing this hand—you have to duck it when it might be a potential trap, and you have to play it aggressively when you think that you either can win the pot uncontested or when you believe that you have the nuts.

# HOW TO PLAY K-Q

Limit hold'em is a big-card game—K-Q is a hand with two big cards. If the flop comes king-high or queen-high, you will have the second-best kicker at all times. And if the pot wasn't raised before the flop, you can be fairly sure that an A-K or A-Q isn't out against you, so the K-Q ought to be the boss hand. It might come with both of them or it might even come A-J-10 or J-10-9, which would be terrific for your hand. As always, the nature of your opponent matters once the action starts after the flop.

## When You Have K-Q in Middle to Late Position

When you're sitting in a middle position or later, you can raise before the flop with a K-Q. If no more than one player has limped in front of you, you can raise the pot—there's a good possibility that you have the best hand. If you raise before the flop and a player reraises behind you, you can call, particularly if the K-Q is suited. A lot of players reraise with J-J, 10-10, and 9-9, and if you have been observant and know that you're dealing with someone who will raise with those types of hands, you're only an 11 to 10 underdog to catch one of your overcards, so you call the raise. If you don't flop to the hand, you can fold.

Now let's say that you limp in with K-Q preflop and someone raises. You can call the single raise, but if an ace hits the board on the flop you're through with the hand. Now suppose you're sitting in a late position and a solid player in early position raises the pot preflop. Just throw your hand away, since you have nothing invested in the pot. If you throw K-Q away preflop every time you're in this situation, you'll be ahead of the game.

## ACTION HAND 91

### Playing K-Q in the Big Blind

Suppose you're in the big blind with the K♣ Q♥. A player raises and two people call the raise. You can make the call for the single extra bet since you know that nobody can reraise behind you. But unless you hit a big flop to your hand (A-J-10 or K-Q-5, for example), you're probably done with it.

Now suppose you're in the big blind with the K♣ Q♥ and the pot was not raised before the flop. The flop comes:

**YOUR HAND**

**FLOP**

In an unraised pot you can be pretty certain that you have the best hand, so you can lead with it. You want to prevent anybody playing low connectors from catching an inside straight card such as a 5, 4, or 3. And you don't want the board to pair either the 6 or the deuce on the turn, which can happen if you allow your opponents to have a free card when they're sitting there with second or third pair. So, you lead at it—if your opponents want to chase, let them do it. The idea is to get the most money you can, so you don't check these types of hands.

> **KEY CONCEPT**
>
> The worst time to check top pair is when you flop one pair.

The worst time to check top pair in hold'em is when you flop a one-pair hand. There's a good chance that you could win the hand with a bet, but instead you check, your opponents check behind you, and they all get a free card. Then they hit their second pair on the turn and you're in trouble. Some players check top pair because they don't want their opponents to know where they're at in the hand. They think it's good to be deceptive so that they can get them for the double bet on the turn. Wrong!

King-queen definitely is a playable hand in limit hold'em, but you have to be very careful with it. Any time you have raised before the flop with K-Q and one or more players have called the raise, you must be willing to release the hand if an ace hits on the flop.

## ACTION HAND 92

### When You Flop Middle Two Pair

Suppose you have the K♣ Q♥ in middle position, two players come into the pot in front of you preflop, and you also just call. The flop comes:

## YOUR HAND

## FLOP

Since the pot was not raised preflop, if someone bets into you, you have to call with your two pair.

But what if the pot was raised before the flop and you called the raise? You must be very careful with your two pair on the flop. Make your best decision before you make the first call. If an opponent leads at the pot, your two pair may not be any good, meaning that it's possible that you have only two outs. For example, if an opponent has an A-K or A-Q, you're playing to catch the opposite card, the only card that you have that is live. Or he might have J-10 for the straight. Actually, you have more outs drawing against the straight than you have drawing against A-K or A-Q. You have two kings and two queens that you could catch on the turn or river to fill up and beat the straight.

If the flop comes K-Q-10 or K-Q-J and it's a raised pot, you also have to be very cautious. You have two pair, but in a raised pot there's a very good chance that you're up against a straight or a set on the flop. Now let's look at a different situation.

## ACTION HAND 93

### Playing Top Two Pair on the Flop

You were the first one in the pot preflop with the K♣ Q♥ and three other players entered the pot behind you. The flop comes K♠ Q♦ 6♣. You're first to act, so you bet your hand and get a couple of callers. The turn card is an ace:

**YOUR HAND**

**TURN**

Anybody who has a J-10 would have called your flop bet with the open-ended straight draw, and anybody who has an A-K will be there too. If the pot was not raised preflop, lead at the pot on the flop—your opponents will let you know where you stand. But if the pot was raised before the flop, keep in mind that after calling a raise preflop, a lot of players will also call a single bet on the flop with A-Q or even A-6 hoping to make top pair, two pair, or a flush if their hole cards are suited.

Of course, you can't be afraid just because an ace hits on the turn. At loose tournament tables, it isn't terribly unusual for players with hands like A-8 to call a bet on the flop just to see the turn card—and if an ace hits, they get aggressive with it. This is one more reason why you have to know your opponents.

In some cases when an ace hits the board on fourth street and a good player raises, you know that you're beat and you fold. But against loose players who like to play any-ace, the raise is not as meaningful. When they hit that ace on fourth street, they may think they have the best hand even though they have no kicker. If you understand the type of player you're against, you can make your best decision.

We can advise you about a lot of situations in these books, but you still have to develop and use insight about who is doing what, when, and why. Know what's going on at your table at all times.

# HOW TO PLAY Q-J

Limit hold'em is a big-card game, as we've said again and again, and queens and jacks obviously are big cards. But Q-J usually is *not* a raising hand in most positions—it is a limping hand only. If the pot has been raised in front of you, just throw the hand away. But if several players have limped into the pot in front of you, you have two choices—you can just call or you can fold. There are several scenarios in which you could flop a big hand to Q-J, but it's still not a raising hand. However, if everyone has passed to you and you're either the first one in or you're in the cutoff seat, you can consider raising against players who will often fold their blind hands.

---

**KEY CONCEPT**

Think of Q-J as two random big cards, and play it that way.

---

## ACTION HAND 94

### When You Flop Top Pair

Suppose you have the Q♣ J♠ in an unraised pot and the flop comes:

### YOUR HAND

### FLOP

In an unraised pot, if you hit either the queen or the jack on the flop you have a decent kicker, though not a great one. If the flop comes with a broken board such as the one pictured here, you can play it stronger than you could against a different type of flop (Q-10-8 or J-10-4, for example). If you bet on the flop and get raised, you have to make a decision as to whether you want to go any further. It is unlikely that the raiser would have two pair (J-4 or J-2) or an overpair (since the pot was not raised before the flop), but he may have a better kicker (A-J or K-J), or a set (if he limped into the pot with pocket fours or deuces, for example). In many low-limit hold'em tournaments, people forget about the importance of a kicker when they flop top pair.

## ACTION HAND 95

### When You Flop Top Two Pair

Now suppose you're playing in a multiway, unraised pot and the flop comes:

**YOUR HAND**

**FLOP**

You have top two pair, so obviously you're going to play the hand strongly. But suppose the board comes:

**FLOP**

You're in trouble anytime you have K-Q and the flop comes with Q-J-10, K-Q-J, or A-Q-J. Even if it comes Q-10-8, there is a potential straight on board since some players like to play hands such as J♠ 9♣. Any time the board has straight potential, you have to be careful about how you play Q-J when you flop two pair.

**CARDOZA PUBLISHING**

# 20 WINNING WITH MEDIUM CONNECTORS

You always want to have the best hand and make your opponents try to draw out on you. You don't want to have the worst hand trying to draw out on an opponent, which is usually the case with medium connectors such as J-10, 10-9, and 8-7, the three hands we discuss in this chapter. If you put your opponents in the bind of having to draw out to beat you, you always have the edge—you don't want to be the one who is going up against the edge. Remember this basic maxim of poker when you're playing J-10 or 10-9: If the pot is raised before it gets to you, you haven't lost a thing by not calling. You will get two new cards the very next deal, so how hard is it to throw the hand away?

## HOW TO PLAY J-10

In the early days of poker there was a lot of conversation about J-10 suited being a great hand. Thus far in this book, all of our big-card hands have been pictured unsuited, because we want to emphasize that you should put more value on the ranks of the cards than on their suits. The same goes for J-10 suited or unsuited, the highest medium connectors you can play. The myth that J-10 is such a strong hand is especially transparent when the pot has been raised. A lot of players who believe that

J-10 is a super hand, suited or unsuited, forget that even a lowly Q-6 offsuit has you beat.

If you flop either a jack or a 10 as top pair, you don't have much of a kicker, do you? The J-10 also can be a trap hand when you catch certain types of flops. For example, suppose the flop comes 9-7-3, giving you two overcards and a middle-buster straight draw. A lot of players get themselves pot-stuck in this type of situation and wind up losing a lot of money to the hand.

In a raised pot, you usually fold with J-10. If the pot has been raised and called before it gets to you and you have a suited J-10, you are a definite dog in the hand—being suited does not increase the hand's value enough to warrant calling a raise cold. Even if the pot has been raised and nobody else calls between you and the raiser, you're still a dog. If the raiser just has two deuces, you're only about even money against him with your J-10 offsuit. Not many people raise with pocket deuces, but the point is that against any underpair, you're about an 11 to 10 dog.

The real strength of J-10 is the 10. A straight cannot be made without a 10 or a 5, so the strength of J-10 is the number of straights that can be made with it. You can flop a lot of different made straights to this hand, plus the straight draws that you can flop to it.

The J-10 is a hand to be played, yes, but it is one that you must play very carefully under the right conditions. You don't want to give it too much credit because it has definite liabilities. Some of the right conditions for playing the hand are:

1. In multiway, unraised pots when you are in late position;
2. When you are defending the big blind for a single bet.

Obviously if you flop two pair, jacks and tens, you have a pretty good hand. But suppose you called a raise before the flop with J♠ 10♥ and the board comes:

### YOUR HAND

### FLOP

Now what are you going to do? Or suppose the flop comes:

### FLOP

On a flop like this, you can sometimes take off a card to try to make the inside straight, but the chances of hitting those middle busters are slim. Also, you can't call a bet in these situations if players sitting are behind you because they might raise.

Although you seldom raise with J-10 before the flop, it still is a hand that is a part of the big-card family. If someone raises in front of you, don't cold call the raise with J-10 (although a lot of players do), because you know that you have the worst of it—and who wants that?

J-10 is a hand to play when the pot has *not* been raised and you are in late position. If you limp in, you can call a single raise and take a flop to the hand. But here's the key to playing J-10: If you don't flop to it, get rid of it immediately. You don't want to get involved in a situation where you flop a jack or a 10, an overcard is on the board, and you continue with the hand—that can cost you a lot of money.

> **KEY CONCEPT**
>
> If you don't catch a good flop to J-10, fold immediately.

If you flop good to the hand, that's another story. You may flop a straight, three jacks, or three tens. Even the K-Q-4 flop might be okay, in which case you can take one card off. We don't suggest continuing with the draw if you don't hit it on fourth street—why pay a double bet for the draw? However, the pot odds come into play in this situation. Even though you don't usually like to play drawing hands in tournaments, you might continue if the pot odds are good enough.

## ACTION HAND 96

### Playing J-10 on a Coordinated Flop

Suppose you have the J♠ 10♠ in late position in a four-way pot. The flop comes K♣ Q♦ 4♠.

You have an open-ended straight draw and a three-flush to go with your J♠ 10♠. In this case you can draw to the hand.

Let's say that you don't make the straight on fourth street, but you pick up a flush draw with the to go with it. The turn card is the 7♠. In this case, you can continue with the hand. But if you make a pair on fourth street against the K-Q-4 flop, you have a big decision to make. Say that the turn card is a jack and the board now reads:

**YOUR HAND**

**TURN**

Obviously the jack might have made a straight for someone else, while you have bottom pair, a four straight, and a four flush. An opponent could already have an A-10, 10-9, or even A♠ 4♠. At the most you would be drawing for a tie if you hit a 10 on the river, but you would be drawing dead to the A♠ 4♠ if any spade comes.

## When it's Late in the Tournament

Suppose it is late in the tournament with only two short-handed tables still in action. At this stage, hands like K-Q, Q-J and J-10 increase in value. Our discussion so far has applied to full-ring action, but as the tables get shorter, these big-card hands increase in value. When you're playing nine-handed at a table, eighteen cards have been dealt. When you're playing five-handed, only ten cards have been dealt, moving your high cards up the ladder.

Just remember that you want to flop something nice to the J-10—you sure don't want to put yourself in a position where you can get killed with it. In tournaments, this is the type of hand that can cost you all of your money. Let's say that you call a bet before the flop—you might even call a raise before the flop—and you flop some possibilities. So you call another bet on the flop, you don't make it on fourth street, and now you have to decide whether to continue. Your thinking might go something like this: "Well, I've already lost two bets before the flop and a bet on the flop. Now it's going to cost me a double bet on the turn. Should I pay for it or not?" Then you rationalize, "Hey, I've got so much money in the pot already, I'm gonna continue." That's bad poker. Take your loss and move on to the next hand.

Now suppose the action is multiway and the pot is huge. You'll probably take the card off and go on to fifth street with the hand because you have the possibility of winning a big-big pot and, because the action is multiway, you have proper pot odds. But if you're playing heads-up or against only two opponents, the odds are so against your making the hand that chasing the money in the pot just isn't reasonable.

Multiway pots tend to come up earlier in the tournament when you're gambling at a lower level; very seldom do you see them in the late rounds. This is a factor to consider with drawing hands—and J-10 is a drawing hand from the get-go. You don't have much to start with, you only have a jack-high hand, and any overcard is a favorite over the J-10. Enough said?

# HOW TO PLAY 10-9

If you are in late position with a lot of chips, and several players have limped into the pot, 10-9 might be worth calling with. If you catch a good flop, you may be able to take somebody off with the hand. But it isn't a raising hand, suited or unsuited. 10-9 is a very tenuous hand, just two cards that you might draw to once in a while from late position to see what happens.

Of course, you also can play it from the blinds in unraised pots. When it costs you only half a bet extra in the small blind or nothing at all in the big blind, 10-9 can be a very nice hand because there are a lot of flops that will help it—but there also are a lot of flops that can hurt it.

## ACTION HAND 97

### When You Flop Top Pair

Say that someone raised the pot before the flop and you called the raise with 10♦ 9♣ on the button. The flop comes:

**YOUR HAND**

**FLOP**

Because the pot was raised before the flop, pocket aces, kings, queens or jacks could be out against you. Also, an A-10, K-10, Q-10, and J-10 all beat you. You have flopped top pair, but you have no kicker! Always remember that a kicker is a big item in hold'em. "When I first started playing," T.J. admitted, "I thought that when I had any ace, I really had a hand, but all I had was a loser. It took me all of a week to learn that kickers are important."

**KEY CONCEPT**

Kickers are very important in limit hold'em.

# HOW TO PLAY 8-7

If you have a lot of chips or a medium stack and your hand is only 8 high, it's a chip burner. Even if you're playing an 8-7 against a short stack, there's a pretty good chance that he can beat an 8-high hand, so you're taking the worst of it. Instead of breaking your opponent, you're giving him a chance to double up.

There are very few conditions in which you can play a hand like 8-7 suited in a tournament:

1. You can play it in the small blind for an extra half-bet in an unraised pot;
2. You can call a single raise in the big blind—if you have a lot of chips and it's multiway action;
3. You can play it on the button for one bet when several limpers already are in the pot.

The 8-7 suited is virtually unplayable in early to middle position. If you're in late position and a few limpers are in the pot, that's a different story—now you have position. You need to have at least two callers in front of you to play the hand, even when you're next to or on the button. If you get a good flop, obviously you can play it further.

You have to get a perfect flop to a hand that's only 8-high, otherwise it just eats up your chips. For that reason, it just isn't a hand that you usually want to play in a tournament. What you really want to play in tournament poker are hands that you *don't* have to get a perfect flop to—which is a big difference between tournament and ring-game play. You don't want to take any heat with this type of hand. This principle also applies to other suited connectors such as 9-9 and 7-6.

However if you are extremely short-stacked and have a chance to enter a multiway pot, you might call a raise with the 8♥ 7♥ and even put in the rest of your chips with it, but only because you're in bad shape anyway. Also, it is unlikely that other people are playing the same kinds of cards in a raised pot, so your hand might be live. You are playing for the added value that comes with a multiway pot; in other words, if you are extremely short-stacked, you might gamble with this hand if you can get a good price.

Some players don't mind taking a shot at the blinds with middle connectors like 8-7 when they're in late position and are the first one in the pot, especially if the blinds are either exceptionally conservative or running desperately low on chips. They rationalize playing this kind of hand by thinking, "I've got some chips and I have a chance to break this guy." We do not recommend this type of play, and here's why.

Suppose you're playing $300/$600 late in the tournament and you have $5,000 in chips. If you raise in the late stages with hands like 8-7 suited, you're burning up your chips, and if you do that two or three times, you might find yourself suddenly down from $5,000 to $3,000. "I wonder where my chips went?" you ask. "I haven't made any bad plays." But you have, so let your opponents make those kinds of plays, not you.

It isn't your job to knock people out of the tournament. You only have to knock one player out—the last one. To expand this concept, imagine a player has J-2 in the big blind in a $500 limit hold'em tournament. The blinds are $1,000/$2,000 and somebody who only has $4,000 in chips pushes all of them to the center in an all-in raise. Everybody passes to you in the big blind and you say to yourself, "It's only gonna cost me $2,000 more, so I'm gonna call and try to bust him." This is one of the worst plays in tournament hold'em. It isn't your job to break him. It isn't your job to lose an extra $2,000 on a hand that you had no business playing in the first place, yet I see so many players doing it.

### KEY CONCEPT
You only have to knock one player out in a tournament—the last one!

When you're tempted to play those kinds of hands, always ask yourself, "Do I want to put my money in with the best hand, or do I want to have to draw out to win the hand?" That $2,000 might be worth $8,000 in a later hand when you have good cards with three callers in the pot with you. But if you lose that $2,000 you don't have it to win their $6,000. And that can make the difference when you get deep into the tournament.

# WINNING WITH MEDIUM PAIRS

When we talk about big pairs, we mean A-A, K-K, Q-Q and J-J. Medium pairs are tens, nines, and eights; and small pairs are deuces through sevens. Of course, there isn't a big difference between eights and sevens, but all the same, the bigger the pair the better off you are.

## HOW TO PLAY 10-10

Two jacks is what we consider to be the median hand in limit hold'em; that is, it's about even money whether one or more overcards flop. But with two tens, you're the "favorite" to see one or more overcards hit the board. This doesn't mean that you should not play pocket tens just because you're afraid of the flop—two tens actually is a very playable hand in a lot of situations. But it isn't playable at all in others—for example, when the pot has been bet, raised, and reraised preflop by solid players sitting in early positions. In this scenario, generally consider passing pocket tens unless everybody comes into the pot and you get a huge price, knowing that you probably would need to flop a set to have a chance at winning the pot.

The only advantage that two tens have over some of the other pairs is that you always need a 10 or a 5 to make a straight, and with 10-10 in your hand you have a little more straight potential. In our opinion, two tens have the best chance of holding up against one or, at most, two opponents. If the pot is played multiway, you almost always have to flop a set or make a lucky straight to win.

## When You're in Early Position

If you are in early position, you usually can bring it in for a raise, and when you are the first one in the pot from middle position on, you *always* bring it in for a raise (and in this case, we do mean always). Remember that after three or four people in front of you have passed, it's an automatic raise.

If one or two players have limped into the pot, it's usually best to just flat call to try to see the flop cheaply. If you are playing in a super loose game where everybody sees a lot of hands before the flop—especially in the early stages of a rebuy tournament (during the rebuy period) when most people at your table are doing a lot of preflop gambling—you may just limp in from early position with pocket tens in order to mix up your play a little bit in the hope of flopping a set. You are not limping to slow-play the hand—two tens is not a big enough hand to slow-play—rather, you limp in because you expect to get multiway action anyway, and because players at these loose tables don't respect early-position raises during the first rounds of the tournament. Realize that if you raise and get four or five callers, you probably will have to flop a set, so you might as well see the flop cheaply. But that no longer is the case from middle position on.

## When You're in Middle Position

When several people already have passed to you in middle position, it isn't shaping up to be a multiway pot like it could be if you just limped in from early position. So, when three or four people already have passed and there's nobody in the pot yet, you want to put as much pressure on the pot as you can before the flop. Players will know that they're not getting a price on their hands. A lot of times, people will play a hand that they think they're getting a price on that they won't play in a much shorter field. You are trying to narrow the field by getting players to lay down hands such as A-3 suited.

If you're playing a freeze-out tournament where everybody plays a bit more conservatively in the early stages, which usually is the case in tournaments with no rebuys, you usually will bring it in for a raise.

## When You're in Late Position

If you are in late position and someone sitting to your right in middle to late position is the first one in the pot and brings it in for a raise, you generally want to reraise to try to isolate him and get the action heads-up. Your equity goes up if you can drive everybody else out of the pot. You probably have the best starting hand, and you will have position on the raiser. If he reraises, just flat call and make a decision after you see the flop. Obviously, if you flop a 10 you have a powerful hand. Your main concern then becomes deciding how to extract the most money you can from your opponent. Usually the later the position that the initial raise comes from, the less strength the raiser needs to bring it in for a raise.

A lot of people in that position raise with hands like pocket eights, nines, A-8 suited, or two high cards such as a K-J or Q-J. If somebody at your table has those cards, your pockets tens are a slight favorite, and you have superior position. If two overcards to your pair come on the flop, you can get away from the hand cheaply. Of course, the raiser might have a big pocket pair—there are no guarantees in tournament poker. You just have to make the best decisions possible—which you're rewarded for in the long run.

# HOW TO PLAY 9-9

When you're playing a tournament and look down at a pair of nines in the hole, the number of players at your table affects your strategy. Raising out of the big blind with two or three limpers in the pot is something that you would not do at a full table—you would rather see the flop cheaply with several limpers already in the pot. But late in the tournament when the table is short-handed with only five or less players, you can raise from the big blind if somebody has limped in before you because you probably have the best hand. In fact, you might even raise from first position at a short-handed table.

## When You're in Early Position

Although you can play 9-9 aggressively at a short-handed table, you cannot play the hand strongly at a full table. When you're playing in a full ring, two nines is a very tricky hand to play from up front. It's a little too good to throw away, but it's also very vulnerable in an early position with so many opponents yet to act. J-J, 10-10 and 9-9 are in about the same category. A pair of jacks is around 50-50 to catch one or more overcards on the flop and, of course, a pair of nines is weaker than that. In early position you might just limp in with the nines because you want to see the flop cheaply.

## When You're in Middle Position

Suppose you have 9-9 in middle to late position and three or four people have passed to you. When you are the first player in the pot, you might bring it in for a raise unless you have a strong feeling that someone is ready to tramp on you with a reraise.

You must be smart enough to get away from nines on the flop. One of the cardinal sins of hold'em is to bet after everyone's checked to you when the flop comes with two or more overcards to your pocket pair. Why not take the free card? Because if you bet and are check-raised, you're in trouble—you have to give up the hand immediately and wind up losing a bet when it didn't have to cost you anything to see the turn card. However, if just one overcard comes out on the flop, you can bet if it is checked to you.

## When You're on the Button

Suppose you're on the button with pocket nines and two or three players have limped into the pot. You can either just call, or you can raise. Let's look at the pros and cons of each choice.

1. **Call.** You usually would just call. Why? Because if you raise, the limpers probably are going to call the single raise—and the types of hands that they limp with are often the connecting cards such as Q-J or J-10, all overcards to your nines. It is possible that you might force out the blinds with a raise, but that's not certain to work.

2. **Raise.** Two nines is a hand that is past the "halfway point" (a pair of eights) and, of course, is better than all lower pairs. You know that you're probably starting with the best hand and it only costs you one extra bet to raise. You also know that most or all the limpers are going to call you. You're building the pot and hoping to win a decent haul with the nines, realizing that you can get away from them if overcards hit the board on the flop. In that case, the limpers will often check to the raiser, giving you a chance at a free card by also checking. Nothing says that you have to play the hand past the flop if it comes with overcards.

Now let's say that you're in the cutoff seat or on the button with only one weak limper in the pot. In that case, you definitely want to raise to get heads-up against one opponent.

Here's another scenario: It's late in the tournament and you're playing high limits. You're on the button with two nines in the hole. Two limpers have entered the pot in front of you. In this situation, there's a good chance that you might just throw the nines away. You're thinking, "We're playing at a high level and I don't want to risk $3,000 on this hand if overcards pop out on the flop. I just have a feeling about this hand." So you slide your nines into the muck. Any time you throw away a decent pair, remember that although you didn't make money on the hand, it didn't cost you anything either.

# HOW TO PLAY 8-8 AND 7-7

If the pot has been raised and reraised before the action gets to you, pocket eights or sevens usually are not hands that you want to play unless five or more player have already called. If the pot will be played with a big field, you don't mind gambling with the middle pairs in the hope of flopping a set, especially if you are short-stacked, because you're getting good odds on your money. In that event, you might even cap it with your case chips since you are getting four or five to one on your money. Naturally this means that you are in late position, because otherwise you can't be sure that the pot will be played multiway.

With your case chips in the pot, even if overcards come on the flop, you will at least get to see all five community cards. You aren't capping the pot because you think that 8-8 or 7-7 is the best hand against four or five opponents before the flop— you're capping it because you're getting a good price for the hand and you're in bad shape. You're willing to gamble, hoping to get lucky and get back in the tournament. Even if you lose, what have you lost? You were short-stacked anyway, so you really haven't lost that much.

So, there are times when you can be aggressive with pocket sevens or eights and take your chances with them—namely, from late position or sometimes from middle position. If you are up against fairly conservative players and no one has entered the pot, you can bring it in for a raise from late position. Raising from a middle position is a more dangerous move, as there are still several people to act behind you.

If you are playing at a fairly loose table, it's a marginal decision as to whether to bring it in for a raise. The tighter the table, the more likely you are to raise. If you are the first one in from a later position, you can almost always bring it in for a raise because two eights figures to be the best hand in that situation.

## ACTION HAND 98

### When You Flop an Overpair & a Straight Draw

Your best scenario with middle pairs is flopping a set. The next best flop would give you an overpair with a straight possibility. Suppose you're in late position with the 8♦ 8♥ and two people have limped. You raise the pot, and the big blind and the two limpers call. The flop comes:

## YOUR HAND

## FLOP

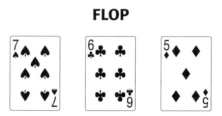

You have flopped an open-ended straight draw to go with your overpair of eights. Of course, with so many players in the pot, an opponent may have an even better hand: a made straight or trips, for instance. Even so, you can be fairly aggressive with the hand to the river.

When you flop an overpair with pocket eights (or lower pairs) *without* an open-ended straight possibility, you're in trouble when the flop comes coordinated. For example, suppose the flop comes:

## YOUR HAND

## FLOP

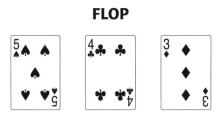

Low connecting boards like this can give someone a straight on the flop, a straight draw, a set, or two pair. So, even when you flop an overpair with your pocket eights, you have to use caution and judgment in how you play the hand, particularly if someone has shown a lot of preflop strength. In that case, you may be up against a larger overpair. For example, say that you're in late position with pocket eights and decide to call a preflop raise by a solid player. If the flop comes something like 7-4-2, you might think that you have the best hand, but in fact you may be up against a pair higher than your eights. As always you have to play the player as well as the hand.

If the action is checked to you after the flop, you can fire a bet at the pot, especially if your eights are an overpair to the flop. Even if there is an overcard to your pair on the flop, you can bet aggressively so long as you think you have the best hand. For example, suppose only the blinds have defended your late position raise and the flop comes:

## YOUR HAND

## FLOP

With only one overcard, you can consider it a favorable flop and bet if it's checked to you. If you get check-raised, you will have to make a decision as to whether your opponent is check-raising with a jack or any other better hand than yours, or whether he is check-raising with two big overcards, or even a 7. In other words, is he raising because he has a hand, or because he thinks you missed the flop?

## ACTION HAND 99

### Playing a Set on a Coordinated Board

Suppose you have the 8♠ 8♣ in late position in an unraised pot. Five of you see the flop, which comes:

## YOUR HAND

## FLOP

How do you like this flop? You like it, but it's still dangerous. Anyone playing a Q-9 has made a straight and anyone with K-Q has a premium straight draw. You can continue to play your set aggressively until you have reason to believe that someone has a better hand than your trips. If another straight card comes on the turn and there are two or three other people in the pot, most of the time you should shut down. You don't necessarily fold because the pot is usually big enough by then to give you proper odds to try to fill up. If someone bets into you, just flat call.

Of course, there's another danger to consider: If the board pairs with a jack or a 10 and someone is playing a J-10, his full house is bigger than yours. If it is checked to you, you can bet. If someone bets into you, you can put in one raise; then if he reraises, just flat call. By just calling the reraise, you may lose a few bets with your lower full house, but you won't lose the maximum.

If a fourth straight card comes on the turn and a very tight player who has called the betting on the flop fires a bet at the pot, you probably should give him credit for the straight, especially if the turn card is a queen, as most players will come into a pot with A-K. You can call his bet on fourth street in the hope of filling up on the river, but if you miss, you probably should fold your trips. This is a delicate laydown, especially in tournaments when people are not making a lot of plays at the pots. But against an overly aggressive player, you might consider calling. Even though you don't like your hand that much, a loose or overly aggressive opponent could have a lesser hand with which he has decided to make a move.

Winning with pairs smaller than nines, eights or sevens is even trickier. We'll look at how to play sixes through deuces in the next section.

# 22 WINNING WITH SMALL PAIRS & SMALL CONNECTORS

When you play a pair of sixes or lower, you virtually always see overcards on the flop, so you almost never have an overpair to the flop unless it comes something like 4-4-2. And when overcards don't flop, a straight possibility usually will be out there. Sometimes you even will have a straight draw yourself with the sixes.

As with medium or small connectors, if you play these small pairs (6-6, 5-5, 4-4 and lower) from early position, you obviously are very vulnerable. These are not hands that you want to take a lot of heat with.

## WHEN YOU'RE IN LATE POSITION

You can play small pairs from late position for the minimum bet when there are several callers in front of you. If you limp with a small pair and someone raises behind you, go ahead and call one more bet. But if it gets raised and reraised behind you, the proper play is to fold, unless you get multiway action from four or more players, in which case it is okay to call the double bet in the hope of flopping a set and winning a monster pot. The hand can be quite deceptive if you flop a set to it, and if that happens you can win more money with it than with connectors because the set is better disguised.

If you are on or next to the button and are the first one in the pot, you might take a shot and raise with two sixes, for example. You will weaken the value of your hand by just limping, so either fold or raise. You have the semblance of a hand against two players (the blinds), or at least one of them (the big blind), so you can raise. You're hoping to win it right there, or at least get heads-up with the big blind when you have position on him and hold what probably is the best hand.

# WHEN YOU'RE OUT OF POSITION

Always remember that you have to fold small pairs out of position. Any time you come into a pot from the first five seats in limit hold'em, you had better be able to stand a raise, otherwise you have made a bad play. Yet you see people playing small pairs all the time from an early position. If someone brings it in for a raise in front of weak players, they routinely call. Their thinking is that the raiser probably has A-K whereas they already have a pair and can flop a set to it. They forget about all those pairs that are higher than theirs, or that their opponent might hit the ace or king.

These types of people play "optimistic" poker rather than optimal poker. But it's not optimism that will help you win a tournament—playing the game correctly is what will get you there. And playing the game right says that playing little pairs up front spells t-r-o-u-b-l-e.

Hold'em is a big-card game. If you play sixes, fives, fours, treys or deuces from early position, you're just asking to get beat and lose your money. You absolutely have to hit a set or get some other fantastic flop to win with these little pairs. So, the best formula for playing sixes or lower in the first three or four seats is to think of them as though they were a 3-2—throw them away. Even though you might put your opponent on overcards only, you should still pass these types of hands.

Remember that people play a lot more hands in cash games because the pots are multiway far more often than they are in tournaments, especially online where it isn't unusual to see five or more people in each hand in ring games. They're hoping to hit a set playing small pairs, and there's nothing wrong with that. Just don't do it in a tournament because small pairs usually burn up your money.

# HOW TO PLAY 5-5

Although a pair of fives is a small pair, it has an added value: You need a 5 or 10 to make a straight and you have two of those cards in your hand. So, it can be pretty sweet if you catch a flop such as 4-3-2, which gives you an open-ended straight draw and an overpair. Sometimes you can trap someone who has an ace in his hand, and if you're lucky enough to catch an ace on the turn or river, you've beaten him with your straight. Of course, it's a little bit dangerous if a 5 hits the turn because then you have a set, but an ace or 6 has made the straight. When that happens, your set may trail on the turn but still, you don't necessarily have to give up the hand—just play it with caution.

## ACTION HAND 100
### When You Flop an Open-Ended Straight Draw

Suppose you have the 5♣ 5♦ in a multiway unraised pot. A good flop to your pair of fives would be something like:

## YOUR HAND

## FLOP

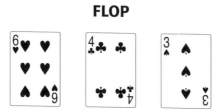

Three players check to you in late position. What's your play? You bet. In this case, pocket fives could easily be the best hand; and even if they aren't, you have a lot of potential to improve to the best hand. Sometimes just hitting the third 5 (which also is the inside straight card) will give you the best hand.

Of course, 5-5 is vulnerable to overcards, so any time that two face cards hit the board you're done with the hand. An exception to this rule of thumb occurs when you're playing against one conservative opponent and he checks to you on the flop. Look at this flop:

## YOUR HAND

## FLOP

In this case you might bet your two fives because there is a good chance that you have the best hand. If your opponent calls, you can reevaluate on the turn. If he is the kind of player that you think he is, he isn't calling because he has a weak jack. He's probably calling with overcards. If a blank comes on the turn and he checks again, you can bet your pair again—but if he check-raises, reconsider your play. The more conservative he is, the more credit you can give him for having a real hand—if he's so conservative, would he really check-raise you if he didn't have a better hand? It's a judgment call. Remember that you're always playing your cards *and* your opponent.

As with all pairs, no matter what their rank, flopping a matching card to your fives is what you're hoping for. Sets will win 80 percent or more of the time when you flop one.

## When You're the First One in the Pot

Playing fives in early to middle position when you're the first one in the pot usually isn't the right thing to do, especially in tournament play, because you can't be sure that you'll get a good enough price for your hand, and because you're out of position, and as a result, very vulnerable. For the most part, then, fold pocket fives out of position unless you're playing in the early stage of a rebuy tournament in which a lot of people are gambling. In that case, you might limp in and hope that you flop a set.

In freeze-out tournaments, 5-5 is a pass from early to middle position. If you're sitting in the cutoff seat or on the button and you're the first one in the pot, you can bring it in for a raise, especially against players who are not liberal blind defenders. If two limpers already are in the pot, you can call a single bet from late position.

If only one limper is in the pot, pocket fives is a pretty marginal hand—unless the limper is very short-stacked and you have a lot of chips. If you are the one who only has a few chips left and he has a lot, you might decide to take a stand with your fives. Or if both you and the limper are very short-stacked, you might play your fives. In any other situation when there is only one limper in the pot, you are better off to pass pocket fives.

# HOW TO PLAY 4-4

Small pairs can be takeoff hands when you have a lot of chips. Keep in mind that 4-4 is only an 11 to 10 favorite over a 6-5. When you take that into account, there are a lot of hands better than two fours. Pocket fives have a little more value because 5 is a straight card.

If you're getting three or four callers in a raised pot and you're sitting around back with a lot of chips, obviously it's nice to have pocket fours. But playing heads-up or even a three-way pot isn't a good idea with little pairs.

While there are certain situations when you can play small pocket pairs, you should usually avoid them. If you stand a little raise in no-limit with a baby pair, it's almost always because you have huge implied odds, lots more chips than the other players, and you're getting multiway action, whereas playing hands like 4-4 heads-up for a raise is almost always a mistake. People who move in with these types of hands are just asking to get broke.

## When You're in Early Position

From a front position, I throw 4-4 away as though it's 7-2. You can only stand a raise with pocket fours if you're getting very good pot odds, and obviously you're hoping to flop a set and rake in a good pot. But if you don't flop a set to your little pair there are very few scenarios where you can play them. In other words, you need to get very lucky to win with small pairs.

Yet time and time again you see players strapped for chips play these hands: A nervous player has $3,000 in chips late in the tournament, looks down at a baby pair, and raises the pot. If he gets called, he's an 11 to 10 favorite at best, but he could also be a 4.5 to 1 dog. And what if he gets reraised? He has to fold, and he's lost a lot of chips unnecessarily. Of course, if you're anteing more than $200 or so, and you only have $800 with the blinds coming up, that's a different situation. In that scenario, you might play the hand, but with $3,000 or $4,000 in chips, you have time to wait for a better hand.

# HOW TO PLAY 2-2

You have to be very selective about the situations in which you play pocket deuces. If you are the big blind, you might call a single raise with pocket deuces, and if you're in the small blind, you might see the flop for half a bet. Usually you want to have two or more people already in the pot. After the flop, you follow the "No set, no bet" philosophy and dump the hand, the same as you do with other small pairs. You don't want to play two deuces from early position if you're the first one in the pot, and if you are in middle position, you don't want to get involved unless two or more limpers already are in the pot.

However, if you are playing a rebuy tournament in the early stage (during the rebuy period), when a lot of people are playing each pot, you might possibly play pocket deuces from up front—but that's the exception, not the rule. In a normal freeze-out event, you must be very careful with them.

## When You're in Late Position

You can sometimes call a raise with pocket twos when you're in late position and know that you're going to get five-or six-way action. For example, suppose a couple of players limp in, another player raises, and one or two people behind him call the raise cold. In this scenario you don't mind gambling if you're in the cutoff seat or on the button, and you can call the raise in the hope of flopping a set.

There are even times when you can raise with pocket deuces, but only when you are the first one in the pot and you're sitting in the cutoff seat or on the button, or when you are in the small blind versus only the big blind—and only against blinds who are not extremely loose players. In this case, there's a good chance that two deuces is the best starting hand, although they're still very vulnerable to overcards.

In tournament play, we use deuces as an example of the smallest pair possible and talk about raising with them as a semibluff, and so on. But late in the tournament when people are just hanging on, trying to survive to the money table, you can raise with *any* hand—it doesn't need to be as "strong" as two deuces.

# WHEN YOU FLOP A FLUSH DRAW

Suppose you're playing a baby pair and flop a flush draw. Drawing to a flush is something that you don't usually consider doing because a higher flush card can so easily beat you—unless you're heads-up against a very aggressive player. If you are in that situation and make the baby flush on fourth street, you might want to call him down if he bets, especially if he's the type of player who will represent a lot of hands. (You certainly can't do that against two or more players because one of them usually will have you beaten.) But what if your aggressive opponent checks to you when the fourth flush card comes out? You probably will only get called if you are beaten, so you just check it down rather than value-bet your hand.

The next hands on our list are small connectors, cards that a lot of limit hold'em players like to play.

# HOW TO PLAY SMALL CONNECTORS

Small suited connectors, of course, are not as strong as the middle suited connectors because many times they make the weak end of the straight. If you have a 5-4 suited, for example, the only time that you have the nuts is when A-2-3, 2-3-6, or 3-6-7 comes. If the flop comes 8-7-6 you can be in a world of hurt with the idiot end of the straight because a lot of players like to play 10-9. So, the higher your connectors, the better off you are.

You can play this type of hand when you are in the small blind and it costs you only half a bet more to see the flop. You also might defend the big blind with small connectors in a multiway pot. Or you may play it on the button or in very late position provided there are at least two other people already in the pot *and* you don't think that the blinds will raise behind you.

# THE TWO LIMPER RULE

This is where the "Two Limper Rule" discussed in *Championship Tournament Poker* comes into effect. The rule goes like this: When two or more players have entered the pot for the minimum bet, a multiway pot is developing. In that case, you will get a nice price to also limp in with suited connectors, small pairs, and other hands that require multiple callers in order to turn a profit. However if you sense that there are too many people yet to act behind you, any one of whom is likely to raise the pot, pass the hand.

It goes without saying (but I'll say it anyway) that if the hand is suited, there is no guarantee that you'll make the best flush with it. A flush is *not* what you're hoping to make with a hand like this.

## ACTION HAND 101

### When You Flop a Flush

Suppose you have the 5♠ 4♠ in late position in an unraised pot. Four players have limped in and you also limp. The flop comes:

**YOUR HAND**

## FLOP

You've flopped a flush—but you're still in danger. Why? Because most players who flop a four flush with a suited overcard in their hand will take a card off to see fourth street at least. Any player who has one single higher card in your suit can make a bigger flush on the turn or river if a fourth suited card hits the board. Therefore, if the fourth flush card comes on the turn, you have to be very careful in deciding whether to continue with the hand.

There are some special situations where you can raise with this type of hand. Suppose it's late in the tournament, you are in late position with a decent amount of chips, and you know that the other players at your table are just trying to hang on for a payout. In these situations it doesn't matter so much what your cards are—with two suited connecting cards you at least can make a straight or a flush with the right flop and ambush the opposition.

This play is one type of semibluff. You have three ways to win:

1. Your opponents surrender without a contest;
2. You outflop them if they call the raise;
3. You could win with a bet on the flop and your opponent folds because he missed.

It's pretty sweet when you've raised the pot with 5-4 from a late position, get there with it, and trap someone with a better hand. I tried this play in a hold'em tournament when I was the first one to enter the pot and held a 5-4. I raised, the big blind flat called my raise with a pair of jacks, and the flop came A-5-5. Needless to say, I took the pot. Just don't count on this ideal outcome every time.

Another type of suited hand that people often play in limit hold'em is a big card suited to a little card, the subject of the next chapter.

# 23 WINNING WITH BIG-LITTLE SUITED

An ace suited or offsuit with a card lower than a 10 is what we call an "any-ace" hand. In loose ring games you'll see a lot of people playing any-ace, particularly if the ace is suited. Then when they enter a tournament they play with that same mentality, particularly during the first three levels of the event. These types of players play very aggressive poker, usually overbetting their hands and giving a lot of loose action. They are the maniacs, the ones who rule the early stages of tournament play—but they aren't around later.

## HOW TO PLAY ACE-ANY SUITED CARD

Any-ace suited is a weak hand, although there are situations when it is playable. You can call with it from the small blind for half a bet in an unraised pot. From the big blind you might call a single raise from a late-position raiser who you know could be out of line. You may also call with this hand when you're in the cutoff seat or on the button in an unraised pot with several limpers already in the pot. In this case you figure that the ace might be good because if an opponent had a big ace, he probably would have raised. And if everyone has passed to you on the button, it's probably correct to raise with an any-ace hand to attack the blinds.

Just remember that if several people have limped into the pot and you call on the button with the A♦ 7♦, the flop you're looking for is two sevens, three diamonds or an ace and a 7. You're not looking to win with a lone ace—if you happen to win with it, that's just a bonus.

## ACTION HAND 102

### When the Flop Comes with an Ace

Suppose you're in the pot with A♦ 7♦on the button. Three or four players have limped in front of you, and you also limp. The flop comes:

### YOUR HAND

## FLOP

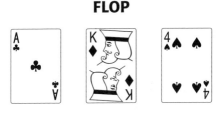

If everyone checks to you, there's a good chance that no one else has an ace. Why? Because A-K, A-Q, A-J are hands that most limit hold'em players either raise with or bet before the flop, and on the flop as well. So you can bet the hand and see what develops. There's a chance that an opponent with a weak ace might have checked because he has no kicker, and someone with a king certainly would've checked with an ace on the flop. If you get check-raised, reevaluate your course of action.

You have to avoid problem hands in tournament poker, and the best way to do that is simply to *not* play them. Certainly avoid playing hands like A♦ 7♦ from the first three or four spots in front of the big blind. Get rid of it so that you can avoid having to make a lot of tricky decisions later in the hand. Actually A♦ 2♦ through A♦ 5♦ is a better hand than A♦ 7♦ in a multiway pot because you can make straights as well as nut flushes with wheel-type aces. Having a 5 along with the ace gives you a straight card for either the wheel or a low straight. If you're going to play an ace with a suited wheel card, play it in the same situations that we have outlined above—calling a half-bet from the small blind, defending the big blind from a late-position raiser, and limping in late position.

However, if that late-position raiser is the guy with a layer of dust on his chips, it isn't worth trying "to keep him honest." You know that either you're a dog with your ace or you have only one overcard. Remember too that you're taking the worst of it trying to hit your suit to win.

## ACTION HAND 103

### Playing Ace/Wheel Card in the Blind

Suppose you're sitting in the big blind with the A♥ 5♥ in an unraised pot and the flop comes:

### YOUR HAND

### FLOP

You have top pair with a weak kicker and a three flush, but poor position. If you're in a multiway pot, check and see what develops. If you are up against just one or two other players, you can bet the hand; if you get played with, reevaluate your strategy after you see the turn card. Sometimes you bet again, sometimes not. It's a judgment call based on your evaluation of your opponents and the texture of the board.

## When You Hit Your Kicker on the Turn

If you hit your kicker on the turn, bet again; if you get raised, just flat call. Don't forget that a card that makes your hand stronger also could strengthen your opponent's hand. Take a look at the board on fourth street:

## YOUR HAND

## TURN

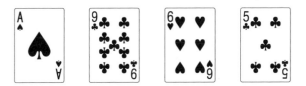

In this example, when you hit your kicker (the 5) and make two pair, one of your opponents could have made a straight if he has an 8-7 in his hand. You also could be up against a bigger two pair or even trips. It is doubtful that either of your opponents holds an A-K because there was no preflop raise. What if another heart comes on the turn? In that case, you would call a bet or raise in the hope of making a flush on the river and taking the pot with the best hand.

# HOW TO PLAY KING-LITTLE SUITED

Time and time again you'll see people play big-little suited cards such as K♦ 3♦, Q♣ 7♣ or J♥ 6♥ in tournaments. And you'll even see players occasionally win with them—but over time, these types of hands will burn up all their chips. Let *them* play the types of hand, but not *you*. A king suited to any small card that is not a connecting card is a bad-news hand. What do you do if you flop a king? You have no kicker.

There are certain situations, however, when you can play a big-small suited hand. For example, you can play K♠ 5♠ in the big blind in an unraised pot, and you might play it in the small blind for a half-bet. Also, if you are in the big blind and a player has raised with his case chips, you might call the raise with a king-small suited to try to beat him *if* no one else has called.

Another scenario in which you might consider playing K♠ 5♠ types of hands is when you're in late position against very conservative players, especially when they're trying to hang on for the money late in the tournament. In that case you might make a raise that is based more on position than on the strength of your hand—you're just trying to muscle them. Of course, you can do that with any two cards—the hand itself might have no value (it could be 3-2 offsuit) because all you're trying to do is steal the blinds.

Although some players routinely play hands like J♥ 6♥ on the button, we do not advise it. When you are tempted to play big-small suited cards on the button, remember what we have emphasized: If nobody has a hand in front of you, there still are two players sitting behind you (the small and big blinds) who might have a real hand. And if one of them does wake up with a hand, you have put yourself in harm's way.

With a king-small, queen-small or jack-small hand, you usually will be drawing to the second, third or fourth-nut flush if two suited cards come on the flop. When you play the A♦ 5♦, your premium hand is the nut flush. With the K♦ 5♦, your premium hand is a high flush—but you could make it and still lose to the ace-high flush. Although the chances that you're up against the ace-high flush are slight, it does happen.

And when it does, it can cost you a ton of chips. In addition to having no kicker, the inferior flush draw is why big-small cards are trouble hands.

One type of gapped hand that is far better to play than big-little suited hands is a one-gap hand. We discuss those types of hands in the next section.

# 24 WINNING WITH ONE-GAP HANDS

Hands with one big card and a side card that is two ranks below it require judgment to play successfully and profitably. Hands such as Q-10 and J-9 fall into this category. Other one-gap hands such as 10-8 and 7-5 require even more skill to play. Being suited always makes a hand more valuable, but suited or not, one gappers are tricky hands to play.

## HOW TO PLAY Q-10

Half of the battle in limit hold'em tournaments is avoiding difficult situations—you don't want to feel like it's a crapshoot when you play a pot. This is why Q-10 should usually be played from late position in unraised pots rather than from early position.

### When You're in Early Position

Pass this trouble hand when you're in early position. In a raised pot, the hand loses a lot of its value, which is one reason why Q-10 is awkward to play from an early position. For example, suppose you call with Q-10 from up front and the action is raised behind you. If you flop top pair to the hand, you cannot know for certain whether you have the best kicker. This makes it a particularly dangerous hand to play in a raised pot. Many people play Q-Q, Q-J, K-Q, A-Q, so when you flop a queen to your Q-10 you're out of position, stuck with a kicker problem, and in a world of hurt. Therefore it's a big losing hand from early position, especially in tournament play because you can't afford to bleed away your precious chips with a hand that has no kicker.

Even from middle position, the hand usually is unplayable, but there's always an exception, of course. If you're in the rebuy period of a tournament and people are gambling, you might try to see the flop cheaply with this hand if you're prepared to mix it up and buy back in. If the Q-10 is suited and there are one or two limpers in the pot, you have more reason to see the flop with the hand. Offsuit the hand is, at best, a marginal call and you must play very cautiously after the flop unless you flop a lucky straight.

## When You're in Late Position

When you're in the cutoff seat or on the button, you might raise with Q-10 if you're the first one in the pot to try to get heads-up with the blinds. If there is only one limper in the pot and you don't think that he is slow-playing a monster hand, you might call from late position with Q-10 but you generally wouldn't raise.

With Q-10 you're looking to flop a straight, two pair, trips, or top pair, and then have everybody check to you so that you can take the lead and feel reasonably comfortable. Of course, if you are check-raised you can't feel at all comfortable with your hand. If you flop trips, you might be in kicker trouble, although you're still going to take your chances with the hand. You'd much rather hit a 10 than a queen, of course.

You may even flop to the hand and still have to fold it. Let's take a look at that type of situation.

## ACTION HAND 104

### Playing Q-10 on a Dangerous Flop

Suppose you've come into an unraised pot from late position with the Q♥ 10♥. The flop comes:

### YOUR HAND

### FLOP

You've flopped top pair with a weak kicker on an extremely perilous board. If you hit your 10 kicker on the turn, an opponent with A-K or K-9 could make a straight. Someone may already have queens and jacks or even a set of fours. If it's bet and raised before it gets to you, you don't have a hand! You simply must fold.

# HOW TO PLAY MIDDLE ONE-GAP HANDS

One-gap hands without a face card are playable under very limited conditions. You can play hands such as 10-8, 9-7, 8-6 or 7-5 from the big blind for a single raise if five or six players are in the pot, since there is no possibility that someone will reraise, in which case you're getting a good price for the hand. You also can play them from the small blind for one half-bet in an unraised pot, but coming in cold for a raise when you are not in the blinds is something that you should not do with 10-8, particularly if there is any preflop heat. You can play these types hands on the button in an unraised pot too, particularly when you know that the players in the blinds usually do not raise preflop.

Naturally, 9-7-6 is a great flop to a 10-8. Another good flop would be J-9-7—unless someone has a Q-10. In that case, he most likely will draw to his open-ended straight, and if he hits either a king or an 8 you probably will lose a few bets to the hand. That is the danger in playing hands like 10-8—you might find yourself up against a higher straight on the turn or river, even if you flop the nuts!

## ACTION HAND 105

### Playing 10-8 on a Dangerous Flop

Dangerous flops occur when you flop top pair with your weak kicker and someone bets very aggressively, especially if the flop has connecting and/or suited cards. Suppose you are in the big blind with 10♦ 8♦ in an unraised pot. The flop comes:

## YOUR HAND

## FLOP

A lot of players these days play hands like A-8 or K-9 suited, and some play one-gap connectors such as 7-5. You could easily be up against a higher pair, a made straight, two pair, or a big flush draw on the flop.

Now let's say that you have 10♦ 8♦ and the flop comes:

## FLOP

When you flop top pair with a 10-8, your 8 is a very weak kicker. Anyone playing an A-10, K-10, Q-10, J-10, or 10-9 has you beat. And again, a player with 7-5 for an open-ended straight draw may be in the hand.

**KEY CONCEPT**

You must be selective and cautious about the conditions under which you play middle one-gappers.

Being suited is always preferable to being unsuited, but that alone is not enough reason to play these hands. You also must have something else going for you, such as being in late position in a multiway pot or being in the blind in an unraised pot.

## When You Have 9-7

Suppose you have 9-7 offsuit. In the big blind you can call a single raise when there are three or four people in the pot, and in the small blind, you can call a half-bet if the pot has not been raised. Or, if the pot has been raised and there are five or six people still in the hand, you might gamble and call the bet from the big or small blind to see the flop. If the raise came from an early-position raiser, you should pass from both the small and big blinds. You need to get a little bit of a price to play this hand—you don't want to go up against an early-position raiser with a hand that is only 9 high.

If you are in middle to late position in an unraised pot, there should be at least two limpers already in the pot because these types of hands are best played in multiway pots. Occasionally, you can raise with 9-7 when you are the first one in the pot and you're in the cutoff seat or on the button. Your intention is to take a shot at the blinds if they are conservative players.

A great flop to 9-7, of course, is 8-6-5, in which case you make the nut straight. You also make a straight with a J-10-8 flop, but you're caught in a dangerous situation. Someone playing Q-9 has the nut straight and anyone playing K-Q is going to be drawing to an ace or 9 to make an even higher straight. As with the 10-8, you can flop a straight with 9-7 and still not end up with the nuts.

If you flop a flush to your 9-7 suited, obviously you have a big hand, unless you're up against a bigger flush. You can play this hand aggressively and hope that another card in your suit does not come on the board, and that the board does not pair, in which case you must let the betting dictate what further action you take. This is where your powers of observation are tested: Will your opponent have the nerve to represent a high flush? Will he represent a full house if the board pairs? You have to make the tough decisions—nothing in this case is cut and dried.

## When You Have 7-5

Suppose you're playing the opening round of a rebuy tournament at the $15/$30 level. Five limpers are in the hand for $15 each, and you are on the button. With all those limpers in the hand, it may be worth your while to put in the $15. If you don't flop to the hand, you can fold it. But you also might get a big flop to it and make a lot of money on the hand. In any other scenario, the hand is worthless. Enough said!

Now, let's move right along to hands with two gaps in them.

# WINNING WITH TWO-GAP HANDS

Be very selective about the situations in which you play two-gap hands such as K-10, Q-9, J-8 or 10-7. Any suited two-gapper must be played under the right set of conditions, thoughtfully and cautiously. Certainly these are not hands that you play in the first two or three positions in front of the big blind—the only suited two-gapper that can be played from early position is A-J. These hands can spell trouble when you play them in a raised pot. Let's discuss each of them separately.

## HOW TO PLAY K-10

This hand has more value if the pot has not been raised. What do people normally raise with? Big cards. Therefore, the hand has more value in late position in an unraised pot. Because people limp in with hands such as K-Q, K-J and A-10, you still have to be cautious even if you flop top pair. If someone fires a bet from early position into a field of four or five people, you don't like your hand that much because there's a good chance that someone has a better kicker.

In tournament play, K-10 is a reasonable hand with which to attack the blinds (if they are conservative players) when you're in late position and are the first one in the pot. In fact, when you're on the button or two spots in front of it, you should think about raising to try to steal the blinds with any two cards 10 or higher—but only when you are the first one in the pot. When you're in late position with one or more limpers in the pot, you might consider limping in for the minimum bet.

Against a solid player who raises from up front, you fold a K-10 even if you are in the big blind and no one else has called the raise. If several people have called the raise, you might consider playing the hand if it is suited, although you generally are better off ducking this hand against an early-position raiser. Ask yourself this: "If Solid Sam has raised from early position and several people have called him, what could the callers have in the hole?" They could easily have K-Q, A-10, K-J, or better.

In that case, if you don't catch a lucky straight or two pair to your K-10, you probably are beaten. This isn't a hand that you can take a lot of heat with. However if an action player raises from a late position, particularly the button, and you are in the big blind with K-10, you generally would call to see the flop.

If you're in the small blind heads-up against the big blind, you can raise with K-10. If one limper is in the pot and you're in the small blind you can see the flop for one half-bet.

## HOW TO PLAY Q-9 AND J-8

You prefer playing this type of two-gap hand against a single opponent. If you do play this type of hand in a multiway pot, the fact that both cards are of the same suit helps, but your flush possibilities could get you in trouble because of the possibility that someone else is holding a bigger flush draw.

You play a hand like Q♠ 9♠ more for its rank and connectedness than for its flush potential. With this sort of hand in a multiway pot, you don't necessarily *want* to make a flush. Any time you play a suited hand that doesn't have the ace in it, you're using it for its straight value or possibly to make two pair or trips. Making top pair usually isn't enough to take the pot.

The value in a hand like this rises in certain circumstances. Suppose somebody raises with A-Q and nobody calls the raise. You're sitting in the big blind with Q-9 suited and decide to call. The board comes Q-9-rag, and just like that, you've trapped the A-Q.

The times that you play these types of hands are:

1. When you're in the small blind for half a bet.
2. When you're in the big blind for a single extra bet.
3. When you're in late position in a multiway pot, preferably unraised.

You do not initiate the action with this kind of hand unless it's blind-against-blind. Or, possibly, when it has been passed to you on the button and you can attack the two blinds. Other than these two situations, you don't initiate the action yourself with hands such as Q♠ 9♠. This is not a hand that you can take a lot of heat with.

# DEFENDING THE BLIND WITH INFERIOR HANDS

Tournament poker players lose a huge amount of chips when they defend their blinds with hands that they would not have played if they were in a different position. Too often they call with a substandard hand, catch a piece of the flop out of position, and wind up losing a lot of extra bets with a hand that they shouldn't have played to start with.

Suppose it's late in the tournament when the blinds are at $500/$1,000. A player with only $2,000 in his stack raises all-in and everyone passes to you in the big blind. You have $10,000 left after posting the $1,000 blind. Do you call the raise or do you pass? A lot of players think that the big blind has to call the raiser, but he doesn't. Calling a raise in situations like this is one of the worst moves that you can make in tournament poker. Although you want to break your opponent, you don't want to lose a lot of chips trying to do it. Why would you want to double up an opponent by playing a bad hand?

But suppose he has $2,000 and you have $30,000. Now it's worth taking a chance to knock him out of the tournament. In this situation you can take a shot at breaking the guy because the worst that can happen if he wins the hand is that he will have $4,000 and you will have $28,000. But when you have only $10,000 and he has $2,000, he will double up to $4,000 if he wins the hand and you will be down to $8,000. Now how do you like it? You have allowed him to get up off the carpet. I can't tell you how many times I've seen someone play a subpar hand because he thought it was mandatory to call, lose the hand, double up his opponent, and then see that same player came back to haunt him later in the tournament.

# HOW TO PLAY A MIDDLE TWO-GAP HAND

Mid-rank two-gap hands such as 10-7, 9-6, and 8-5 are big-big trap hands. You might play one of these hands suited or unsuited from the big blind in an unraised pot, or for half a bet in an unraised pot from the small blind—but if the pot has been raised, you should surrender it from both the big and the small blind. Getting trapped with these hands is your biggest fear. Suppose four players are in the pot for the minimum bet, and you call with the 10♠ 7♠ from the small blind. You flop either a 10 or a 7 for top pair and become involved in the hand. You've caught a little piece of the flop and often, you die with it. Always be leery of "free" hands.

Being suited is always preferable to being unsuited when you play a two-gap hand. But even when they are suited, you usually must have exactly the right set of circumstances before you can play these types of cards. It's difficult to make the absolute nuts with these hands—even when a two-gap hand makes a straight, it's sometimes possible for someone to make an even higher one. If the hand is suited, you prefer to make a straight rather than a flush because of the chances that someone will make a better flush. If that happens, you probably will lose a few bets to the hand.

Generally speaking, you won't play these hands at all, though there are a few exceptions. One of them is when you are in the big blind and your two-gapper is suited. In this case, you can call a single raise if several people already are in the pot. Whether the hand is suited or not, you can play it for a half bet from the small blind when several players already are in the pot. If you don't flop to the hand, it's very easy to get away from it.

If you catch a little piece of the flop, proceed with caution. Even if you flop top pair, the hand is vulnerable, especially with several people still in, because your kicker is bad. You would like to have a straight possibility to go with your pair, which would make your hand stronger. If you flop two pair or a straight, of course, you can be aggressive with the hand.

## When You're in Late Position

With any two cards you can attack the blinds from a late position when it is late in the tournament and everyone is playing super tight, just trying to make it into the money. As a result you can attack with hands like 9-6 and 8-5 when you are the first one in the pot. Actually, it doesn't matter what your cards are—they could be 7-2 offsuit. You're not raising on the strength of your hand, you're just making a play at the pot to steal the blinds when you think that everyone has tightened up their game.

Sometimes you even get a lucky flop to your hand, which is a bonus. Occasionally you're going to hit something. Just remember that mid-rank two gappers are trash hands that you can only play in certain situations.

If playing two-gap hands is dangerous, imagine how perilous three-gap hands can be. That's the subject of our next chapter.

# WINNING WITH THREE-GAP HANDS

Hands with three gaps in them are some of the trickiest hands you can play in limit hold'em, but you'll find a lot of players coming into pots with them. Let's discuss how to play A-10 and K-9 for starters, and then move along to mid-rank three gappers such as 10-6.

## HOW TO PLAY A-10

A lot of people play ace-anything, and against those types of players an A-10 is a reasonable hand. But beware—against solid, reasonable players who raise from early position with quality hands only, A-10 is a trouble hand that you should duck.

If you're in the small blind with A-10, you can attack the big blind with the hand when no one else is in the pot. When you are in the big blind with A-10, you can see the flop against a late position raiser. If the raiser is on the button and is someone who has raised with all sorts of goofy hands, you might consider reraising just to keep him off balance. You don't want him to get in the habit of trying to run over you thinking that you're only going to call his raises.

From late position when you're the first one in the pot, feel free to attack the blinds with A-10. If there is one limper in the pot, particularly if he limps in with a lot of marginal hands, you might consider raising the pot even if you expect him to call the raise. With two limpers already in the pot, it's not a great idea to raise with A-10, suited or not.

When the A-10 is suited it has more value, but in any raised pot, A-10 suited or unsuited must be played with caution. If you are the raiser and get played with, you have to be careful with the hand even when you flop to it. You're hoping to flop a 10 rather than an ace, because you have the boss kicker when you flop a 10. The perfect flop, of course, is K-Q-J because that will hit a lot of people. If someone is playing Q-J, K-Q, or K-J, they have flopped two pair against your made straight, and they probably will have problems getting away from their hands. With two pair, they have four outs, and only three outs—for a tie—if they have a pair and a straight draw.

## ACTION HAND 106

### Playing A-10 on a Trouble Flop

A trouble flop is when you hit a part of the flop and you're not sure where you stand with your A-10. For example, suppose you're in late position with the A♥ 10♥ and the flop comes:

### YOUR HAND

## FLOP

You've flopped second pair. You may have the best hand on the flop, but with two connecting cards on the board, not only are you beaten by someone with a jack, but anyone with a hand such as K-Q or 9-8 has a lot of outs to improve to the best hand and beat you on the turn or river. How do you play the hand against this flop?

You like your hand better if the pot has not been raised before the flop because a lot of times, people automatically check to the raiser. If one of your opponents has a jack (or another top pair) in an unraised pot, he usually will lead at it on the flop, giving you an indication of where you stand. But when the pot has been raised preflop, he probably will check-raise you.

Let's say that you brought it in for a raise preflop from late position and everyone checks to you on the flop. You can bet the hand and see what develops. You can always back off if you get too much heat. But as long as your opponents are playing passively, you can bet the hand again if everyone checks to you on the turn, especially if a non-threatening card comes out. Take a look at this board:

## YOUR HAND

## TURN

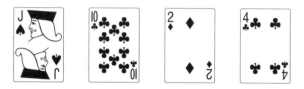

A non-connecting card such as the 4♣ or 6♦ hits on the turn and everyone checks to you. You bet and an opponent check-raises you. What do you do now? You'll have to give the check-raiser credit for a jack because players usually will not risk their valuable tournament chips on a check-raise bluff with one card to come. You usually should fold when someone makes this type of play unless you have some sort of straight possibility to go with your second-pair.

But what if you're up against an action player that you think is capable of making this play without the goods? In that case, you may want to call him down. Another alternative is to just check on fourth street and see what your action opponent does on the river. If he bets, you call. If he checks, you bet.

## ACTION HAND 107

### Playing A-10 on an Ace-High Flop

Another dangerous situation for your A-10 occurs when you flop an ace. When you flop an ace to your A-10, it's always more dangerous in a raised pot. When the pot has not been raised, it is less likely that you're against an A-K, A-Q, or A-J and you're more likely to continue with the hand. How you proceed always depends on the preflop action. Even though there are no exposed cards like there are in seven-card stud, you can gather a lot of information in hold'em. The information that you gather from the preflop action determines how strongly you can play A-10 and how long you stay in when you flop an ace.

For example, when you are playing against only one opponent in an unraised pot, he could easily have a weaker kicker than your 10. He may think that because the pot was not raised preflop, you also have a weak kicker and his kicker has you beat. So, you don't have to automatically abandon the hand if he bets—just hope that he didn't hit his weak kicker on the flop. If he's the type of player who makes a habit of playing ace-anything, you might want to just check-call, gritting your teeth along the way in the hope that he hasn't hit his kicker.

Suppose you decided to take a chance and come into an unraised pot from late middle position with one limper in front of you. The button and the big blind also just called. The flop comes:

## YOUR HAND

## FLOP

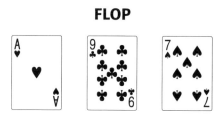

The preflop limper bets in front of you, you raise, and the button cold-calls behind you. It is unlikely that someone has a 9-7 or 10-8 (although it's possible), and, of course, it's possible that someone could be playing a suited ace and has made two pair. But generally, you are more concerned about an opponent having an ace with a bigger kicker.

If you are the first to act you can lead at the pot, but if a player raises behind you, you must reevaluate. Do you want to continue with the hand? If the raiser is a solid player, you can't put him on a draw because you know that he would only raise with an A-J or better. So, you probably should fold.

# HOW TO PLAY K-9

K-9 suited is a typical "temptation" hand. It looks fairly good but it can lead you into a world of trouble. In wide-open hold'em tournaments some people will play king-anything suited, and the 9 gives the hand some straight potential, even though it's a three-gap hand. Of course, when you flop a straight to it, like Q-J-10—you can be beaten by anyone holding A-K.

You must be selective about how you play this hand—it's not one that you can take heat with.

If you're in the big blind and someone has raised the pot with several callers, you can defend your blind for the single raise. From the small blind, pass in a raised pot, but you might call for one half-bet in an unraised pot and see what develops on the flop. Heads-up against the big blind you can raise with K-9, as it figures to be a better hand. When you are in late position and several people have limped in, you can do the same. But against an early-position raiser, K-9 suited is not a playable hand. From early to middle position, whether or not the pot has been raised, this hand is a chip burner.

If you are getting close to the money table, K-9 is not the type of hand that you want to take a risk with if you are low on chips. If you're in a desperate situation—for example, the blinds will eat you up in a few hands—you may want to take a stand with K-9 from late position. Not because you like the hand, but because playing K-9 appears to be a better option than playing the fast approaching blinds all-in.

What if you flop either a flush or a flush draw to K-9 suited? If you flop a flush you should play this hand very aggressively. You are holding the second nuts and generally will win with it. Of course, if the ace and two other cards of your suit come, you have the nuts and can play it accordingly. You can check-call on the flop and then raise on fourth or fifth street, or you can lead and hope to get raised. Play it any way that you think will get the most bets from the table.

If you flop a flush draw, let your position dictate how you play from there. In an unraised pot from early position, check-call if the pot is multiway, and check-raise if you're heads-up. In late position with a decent stack of chips, you usually can raise to create a bigger pot. Your raise usually will get you a free card on the turn because your opponents will often check to the raiser on fourth street no matter what card comes. You have to consider the possibility that someone is drawing to the nut flush, and the play at your table usually will dictate where you stand.

# HOW TO PLAY MIDDLE THREE-GAPPERS

Another three-gap hand that some players like to play when it is suited is a hand such as 10-6 (and even J-7 or 9-5). Although the 10 has some straight potential, this hand falls into the category of two-gap unsuited hands, in that even if you flop a straight to it, someone could have a better straight. For example, suppose the flop comes 9-8-7. Since people habitually play J-10, you could be in a world of hurt with your second-best straight.

When you are tempted to play these types of hands, ask yourself, "What am I hoping to make?" At least with a hand like K-9 suited you can make a high flush, but the best that you can do with 10-6 suited is make a low flush that is vulnerable to higher flushes and a second-best straight. Unless you catch a flop like 10-10-6, you're asking for trouble when you play hands like this.

About the only time that it's playable is for one half-bet in the small blind or the mandatory single bet in the big blind (in unraised pots). If someone raises before you must act from the big blind, the only reason you might call is when five or six people already are in the pot. Even then, it is a questionable call because you must flop perfectly to it. Certainly you don't lose much by passing.

Flopping top pair to 10-6 can be dangerous business. Suppose you're in the big blind in an unraised pot and you flop top pair. Against only one or two opponents you might lead at the hand to see whether it's good. But with more than two other people in the pot, you should check. A lot of people like to play hands that have a 10 in them, so if one of your three or four opponents has a 10, his kicker most likely is higher than your lowly 6.

Sometimes you will see people defending their blind with hands like 10-6 suited against a late-position raiser. But even if the raiser has a weak hand, yours probably isn't any better— and he has position on you after the flop. Why put yourself in the trap of having to make a lot of tricky decisions, especially if you catch a little piece of the flop. Part of the value of this book is to help you avoid these types of situations.

You can really get caught in some tricky situations when you play hands in the blinds, the subject of the next chapter.

# WINNING IN
# THE BLINDS

The most expensive hand you'll ever play in a limit hold'em tournament is the hand you get for free in the big blind, or the one that costs you only half a bet more in the small blind. More tournament players have crippled themselves by defending a blind that they should not have played, or by playing more aggressively than they should from the blind when they flop something marginal, than for any other reason.

---

### KEY CONCEPT

The big blind and the small blind are the most expensive hands you'll ever play in a hold'em tournament.

---

What often happens is that you catch part of the flop and become involved with a hand that you wouldn't have played had you not been in the blind. With a hand such as Q♠ 8♠ your thinking may go something like, "This isn't a great hand, but there are several people in the pot and it's only going to cost me half a bet to call." If a fast or unknowledgeable player flops a queen, he may make the mistake of betting the hand aggressively, when a better option is to just check and see what kind of action takes place behind him. Then if an opponent raises his blind bet, he is faced with a quandary: "Should I call the raise or pass?"

Playing the blinds correctly requires extreme prudence and discretion. Three key factors influence your play:

1. The number of opponents in the pot;
2. The playing styles of your opponents; and
3. The nature of the flop.

If one of your adversaries is the type of player who would raise to try to get a free card if the flop gives him a straight or flush draw, you might continue playing when you flop top pair with your Q♠ 8♠. But if there is no logical draw on the flop other than top pair/top kicker or trips, and if you have no other reasonable outs, you must seriously consider just passing his raise.

Troublesome blind hands are even trickier to play when you catch part of the flop in a raised pot. For example, with a hand such as A♥ 8♥ you must proceed cautiously if you flop an ace. Against any substantial action, you are better off to just give up. The strongest hand that you can hope to flop (aside from a made flush) is top pair with a flush draw. Be willing to go to the river if the flop comes A♦ K♥ 4♥, for example. As long as you are not raised, you can continue to take the lead. However, if you are subjected to any type of substantial action, you may be forced to just check-call. If your flush fails to materialize on the river, you can check and then decide whether to pay off an opponent who bets.

Against a single opponent who has just called all the way, you may as well bet if you intend to call anyway, unless you believe that he might raise you. If you indeed think that he may raise, it would be wise to check to him, thus avoiding being bluffed out of the pot, and also giving yourself an opportunity to snap up the pot if your hand is better than his. Checking on the river sometimes can induce a bluff. Your apparent weakness may tempt your opponent to bet when he actually has been on a draw and holds only a lower pair than you do.

Starting hand requirements with which you can defend the small blind can be more liberal in unraised pots than in raised pots. In raised pots you can call from the small blind with small pairs and suited connectors when five or more people are in the pot, including yourself and the big blind. Suited cards with two gaps and straight potential such as 8♠ 5♠, 9♥ 6♥ or 10♣ 7♣ are also hands that you can play for an additional half-bet, but only when there are several people in the pot.

# WHEN TO RAISE FROM THE BLINDS

Any two cards 10 and higher are worth a raise from the small blind against the big blind, or if you are the big blind and the small blind has only called. Ace-x is worth a raise in a small blind-big blind confrontation, or against a small blind that has limped into the pot. It usually is correct to raise with these hands, regardless of chip count. Just be aware that playing blind against blind is more likely to happen from the middle rounds of a tournament onward than in the opening stages.

Be very hesitant about raising from the small or big blind with multiple players in the pot. Against five or more players, your raise must be based strictly on the merits of your hand. Occasionally, you will see players raise with small to medium pairs. Although raising is a way to build a big pot, you will be forced to flop a set to have your hand stand up in multiway action. Therefore, it makes little sense to raise with these hands unless you're in a gambling mood.

One time that you might raise from the big blind with a small to medium pair is when you are almost broke and several people already are in the pot. With a "What the hell!" attitude, you can fire in your last chips on a raise, knowing that no matter what comes, you'll be getting multiway action on your money with the odds of hitting your set at 7.5 to 1 on the flop and 4 to 1 if you go to the river. With an average stack, you are better off just calling from the big blind, hoping to hit your set. If you are in the small blind with only a few chips remaining, you usually should wait for the button.

# A FINAL WORD

When you're tempted to play a sub-par hand from the cutoff seat or the button, think twice before you push your valuable chips to the middle. The "bunching factor" is an important concept to remember when you're in late position with only the blinds to act. If a lot of people have passed, it is likely that none of them are holding big cards. It then becomes more likely that one of the blind hands does have big cards, so be aware that one of the blinds may wake up with a premium hand in these situations.

Some people cannot be bluffed, although this is a less frequent occurrence in tournaments than it is in ring games. If you think that a player will defend his blind very liberally—he's a "bluff-proof" blind protector—you should base your betting strategy strictly on the merits of your hand, rather than on trying to run over someone who won't lay down a hand no matter what. Trying to bluff a player who is bluff-proof can be a costly tournament error.

In closing, let's turn to a subject that has become more and more important in today's increasingly fast limit and no-limit hold'em tournaments: how to outwit and outplay very aggressive opponents.

# HOW TO PLAY AGAINST SUPER-AGGRESSORS

## TOM MCEVOY

In *Championship Hold'em*, T.J. Cloutier and I defined some of the changes in the way that tournaments and cash games are being played today. One of those changes has been brought about by the playing style of the Super Aggressors, bandits who try to steal your chips even when they don't have a premium hand. They are the ones who constantly put a lot of pressure on their opponents, and they pick up a lot of pots that are "up for sale" when their more conservative opponents show weakness. Super Aggressors are always firing away at these "ownerless" pots and they're winning a fair number of them, because, although their opponents know that they're probably stealing, they don't have enough of a hand themselves to put up a fight.

## WHO ARE THEY?

Super Aggressors play much more aggressively before the flop with a lot of hands—and they aren't always premium. They play position very strongly and don't need as much of a hand to bring it in for a raise, especially when they're the first one in the pot. They either raise or fold, and they three-bet a lot of marginal hands. If a Super Aggressor thinks that someone is out of line with a late position raise, he will come over the top of the raiser, even with hands such as Q-10 or a pair of deuces.

Super Aggressors are also willing to check-raise with nothing, which is very hard to pull off, and requires immense skill. Although this kamikaze style often will cause the Super Aggressor to crash and burn early in the tournament, it also can help him amass a lot of chips if some of his hands hold up.

In multiway pots, the Super Aggressor will gamble with all sorts of strange hands before the flop. For example, he might call two or three bets cold with an 8-6 suited or a small pair—he's willing to gamble in the hope of catching a favorable flop. Super-aggressive players will play any pair, sometimes bringing it in for a raise, and I've seen them cap the pot with hands like 10-10 or K-8 suited.

When the flop comes raggedy, Super Aggressors bet A-K even though all they have is overcards, a strategy that I think is generally a mistake. Suppose there are about five people in the pot and the flop comes 9-4-2 with three different suits. Continuing to be aggressive with A-K in this scenario is a mistake because someone is going to have something. I don't agree with that kind of play, but we have to deal with it in today's faster, more aggressive tournament action.

These Super Aggressors are usually younger than 40, fearless, and aggressive to the point that they either fold or raise with marginal hands (rather than just calling with them). In other words, they aren't playing "by the book." That is, they aren't gauging their play by "Group I" hands, "Group II" hands, position, and so on.

Most of these players play their poker in California. Although Asian players have been typecast as Super Aggressors, there really isn't any correlation to race. Super Aggressors are most likely to intimidate players that are older, more conservative, and less experienced, as well as women. (Note, however, that although women in general are more conservative, some are every bit as aggressive as men.)

# WHY ARE THEY SO DANGEROUS?

The style of the Super Aggressor tends to throw more cautious players off their game by moving them out of their comfort zone. The Cautious Conservative is not comfortable playing in games where people are reraising with pocket fours and 10-8. The aggressive players who fit the kamikaze profile are unpredictable to their more traditional opponents, whose ability to read other players decrease because they can't put their aggressive opponents on specific hands, and wind up giving action when they're beaten.

At the same time, the Cautious Conservatives are *more* predictable with their "A-B-C" style of traditional tournament play. The Super Aggressor, who looks like a wild man to the Cautious Conservative, is able to read his traditional opponents much better than they are reading him, which, of course, is a huge advantage. In fact some Super Aggressors don't have a lot of respect for the older champions and think they can run over their more seasoned opponents.

# ADJUSTING YOUR STRATEGY

So, how can we traditionalists adjust our play to contend with and defend against the Super Aggressors? One thing you can do is to call people down with less strength than you ordinarily would, especially when you're putting them on a hand like A-K and think that they're betting with overcards only. Another play you can make is to check-raise with second pair, particularly when the game is short-handed. For example, suppose you have two tens and one overcard comes on the flop. If a very aggressive player keeps firing at you, you might simply call him down. In the past I wasn't keen on engaging them, but these days I do, and, quite often, I have the best hand.

Since I am known as a more traditional tournament player, I decided it was time to refine my style to better compete in today's more aggressive tournaments. I'm willing to make some adjustments in my play and change my game around if it means getting better tournament results. Specifically, I have experimented by playing online hold'em in $15-$30 short-handed games.

I've been playing a much more aggressive style than I am accustomed to, and although I've had some big swings, for the most part I have made a lot of money by opening up my game and playing a very fast style. I look for short-handed games, something I never used to do. I will deliberately try to find a three or four-handed game, and I'll even start a game heads-up. I've also been trying to profile other online players in an effort to get a line on everybody's play, especially the weaker players. For example, I look for certain players that I know are fast and loose and try to get position on them, avoiding the players that I know are tough and have been very successful in short-handed games.

Are these super-aggressive tournament aces for real? They are, but not everyone can play like they do and get the same results. That's because they're not only aggressive, but also very skillful tournament pros.

Here's the bottom line: If you can't beat 'em, try joining 'em. There's a reason why some of the new breed of tournament players with their super-aggressive style are successful. Yes, they crash and burn more often than not, but when they get there, they get there with chips—and they know how to win. They may have only a few firsts and a lot of last-place finishes, but those firsts are worth a whole lot.

Can today's Super Aggressors sustain their good results over the long haul? The answer is not clear-cut—they've had a lot of success the last few years, but it's hard to tell where they'll be ten years from now.

# TOURNAMENT POKER TERMS

**Any Ace**

An ace with a weak kicker. "Some people will play *any* ace—even an A-6—from late position in a tournament." Also called a "weak ace."

**Backdoor a Flush/Straight**

Make a hand that you were not originally drawing to by catching favorable cards on later streets. "I was betting top pair, but when a fourth spade hit on the river, I *backdoored* a flush."

**Backer**

Someone who pays the entry fees for a tournament player, and then splits the reward with the player at the end of the event. "My *backer* gave me the money for my buy-in and we agreed to split evenly any money I won."

**Backup**

A card that provides you with an extra out. "If you have a drawing hand, you like to have a *backup* to your draw, a secondary draw that might make your hand the winner."

**Beat into the Pot**

When an opponent bets an inferior hand, you gladly push your chips into the pot. "When three clubs came on the flop, Slim moved in. I *beat him into the pot* with my flush—he had a 10-high flush, mine was higher."

**Behind (Sitting)**

You have the advantage of acting after someone else acts. "So long as you're sitting *behind* the other players, you have the advantage of position."

## Big Ace

An ace with a big kicker (A-K or A-Q). "When the flop came A-6-2, I played my *big ace* strong."

## Big Flop

The flop comes with cards that greatly enhance the strength of your hand. "I caught a *big flop* that gave me the nut flush."

## Boss Hand

The best possible hand. "When you have the *boss hand*, you should bet it as aggressively as possible, especially if you think your opponents have drawing hands."

## Broken Board

The board cards are random with no pair, flush, or straight possibilities. "A *broken board* such as 9-5-2 of three suits is a fabulous flop to pocket jacks."

## Bully

To play aggressively. "When I have a big stack in a tournament, I like being able to *bully* the entire table."

## Buy-In

The amount of money it costs to enter a tournament. The cost of the buy-in is often used to describe the size of a tournament. "He didn't have enough money for the *buy-in* to the $1,000 hold'em event, so he sold pieces of his action to three other players."

## Case Chips

Your last chips. "He raised all in with his *case chips*."

## Change Gears

To adjust your style of play from fast to slow, from loose to tight, from raising to calling, and so on. "When the cards quit coming his way, Will didn't *change gears*; instead, he kept on playing fast and lost his whole bankroll."

## Chip Status

How the number of chips that you have in front of you compares to those of your opponents. "With twice as many chips as my opponents, Ray's *chip status* at the final table was excellent."

**Cold Call**

To call a raise without having put an initial bet into the pot. "Bonetti raised, Hellmuth reraised, and I *cold called*."

**Come Over the Top**

Raise or reraise. "I raised it $2,000 and Sexton *came over the top* of me with $7,000."

**Commit Fully**

Put in as many chips as necessary to play your hand to the river, even if they are your case chips. "If I think the odds are in my favor, I will *commit fully*."

**Confrontation**

A big pot that usually is contested heads up and often significantly changes the players' chip status or alters the outcome of the tournament. "When Stu pushed all his chips to the middle, Ron had to decide whether he wanted to get into a big *confrontation* with him at that point in the tournament."

**Cutoff Seat**

The seat immediately in front of the button. "He raised from the *cutoff seat* to try to shut out the button and the blinds."

**Decision Hand**

A hand that requires you to make a value judgment. "Pocket aces and trash hands play themselves. It is the *decision hands* like A-K that will determine your profit at the end of the session, the day, the year."

**Flat Call**

Calling a bet without raising. "When he bet in to me, I just *flat called* to keep the players behind me from folding."

**Flop to It**

The flop enhances the value of your hand. "If you don't *flop to it*, you can get away from the hand."

**Freeze-Out Tournament**

In a tournament, when your original buy-in is gone, you cannot rebuy or add on extra chips to remain in play. "All WSOP events are *freeze-out* tournaments."

**Get into the Deck**

Get a free card. "If you just check your one-pair hand, you allow your opponents to *get into the deck*."

**Get Away From It**

To fold, usually when what appeared to be a premium hand catches an unfavorable flop that negated its potential. "If you don't flop to your hand, *get away from* it."

**Get the Right Price**

The pot odds are favorable enough for you to call a bet or a raise with a drawing hand. "Since I was getting the *right price*, I called the bet with a wraparound."

**Get Full Value**

To bet, raise, and reraise to manipulate the size of the pot so that you will win the maximum number of chips if you win the hand. "By raising on every round, I was able to get *full value* when my hand held up at the river."

**Get There**

You make your hand. "When you *get there*, you might be able to start maximizing your bets."

**Give Them**

You attribute a hand to your opponents. "When the flop comes with a pair and your opponent raises, what are you going to *give him*? A straight draw?!"

**Isolate**

You raise or reraise to limit the action to yourself and a single opponent. "I raised on the button to *isolate* against the big blind."

**Increment**

The increase in chips required to post the blinds and antes at the start of a new round in a tournament. When the blinds rise from $25/$50 to $50/$100, the increment has doubled. "When the *increment* doubled after the sixth level, I decided it would be too expensive to play small connectors."

**Jammed Pot**

The pot has been raised the maximum number of times. "You should pass with a weak hand if the pot has been *jammed* before it gets to you."

**Key Card**

The one card that will make your hand a winner. "I knew that I needed to catch a 10, the *key card* to my straight draw."

**Key Hand**

A hand that turns the tide of fortune in a tournament. "The key hand that put me in a position to win came when I hit the flush at the river and won a huge pot."

**Lay it Down**

Fold. "Many times, you can put enough pressure on the pot to blow everybody away and sometimes even get the raiser to *lay down* his hand."

**Limp**

Enter the pot by just calling. "I decided to just *limp* in with a pair of tens and see the flop as cheap as possible."

**Limper**

A player who enters the pot for the minimum bet. "When there are two *limpers* already in the pot, a pair of jacks should be your minimum raising hand."

**(Two) Limper Rule**

Once two or more people have voluntarily entered the pot for the minimum bet, the hand has already shaped up to be multiway. "Small pairs and connectors become somewhat more attractive in middle to late position when *two or more players have limped* into the pot in front of you."

**Live Cards**

Cards that you need to improve your hand and which probably are still available. "When three players who I knew to be big-pair players entered the pot in front of me, I thought that my middle connectors might still be *live* so I decided to play the hand."

**Long Call**

To take a long time to decide whether to call a bet with a marginal hand. "When making a *long call*, your opponents can get a read on you."

**Make a Deal**

To negotiate a way of dividing the money among the top finishers at the last table in a tournament. "When we got to heads-up at the final table, John and Mary *made a deal* to split 90 percent of the prize money and play to the end for the other 10 percent of it."

**Make a Move**

To try to bluff. "When the board paired sixes, Max *made a move* at the pot. I thought that he was bluffing but I had nothing to call him with."

**Middle Buster**

An inside straight draw. "If the flop comes A-10-4 and you have the Q-J, you're not going to draw to the *middle buster* to try to catch the king."

**Nut Draw**

You have a draw to the best possible hand. "When two clubs come on the board and you have the A] J], you have the *nut* flush *draw*."

**Nuts**

The best hand possible in any given pot. "Remember that you can flop the *nuts* and lose it on the turn; for example, when you flop the nut straight and the board pairs making a full house for your opponent."

**Nutted Up**

When someone is playing very tight. "Jackson was so *nutted up* at the final table, I stole pot after pot from him."

**Out**

A card that completes your hand. "Always try to have an extra *out*, a third low card to go with your ace, when you're drawing for the low end."

## Overpair

A pair in your hand made up of cards higher than the highest card showing on the board. "When the board came Q-J-6, I had an *overpair* with my pocket kings."

## Pay Off

To call an opponent's bet at the river even though you think that he might have the best hand. "When the board paired at the river, I decided to *pay him off* when he bet because I wasn't sure that he had made trips."

## Payout

The prize money you win at the end of the tournament. "Coming in first, James won a *payout* that was double the amount of second place."

## Peddling the Nuts

Drawing to, playing, and betting the nut hand. "Players may not always be peddling the nuts in a heads-up situation, but in any multiway pot somebody's usually drawing at the nuts if he doesn't already have it."

## Piece Yourself Out

To raise your tournament buy-in by selling shares of your potential winnings. "I had *pieced myself out* three ways, so I didn't have a huge payday."

## Play Back

Responding to an opponent's bet by either raising or reraising. "If a tight opponent *plays back* at you, you know he probably has the nuts."

## Play From Behind

Checking with the intent of check-raising when you have a big hand. "I knew that Kevin usually *played from behind* when he had a big hand so when he checked, so did I."

## Play Fast

Aggressively betting a drawing hand to get full value for it if you make it. "Many players *play fast* in the early rounds of tournaments to try to build their stacks."

**Play Slow**

The opposite of playing fast. To wait and see what develops before pushing a hand. "When you make the nut straight on the flop and there's a chance that the flush draw is out or possibly a set, why not play your hand *slow* to start with?"

**Play With**

Staying in the hand by betting calling, raising, or reraising. "You should realize that you're going to *get played with* most of the time because hold'em is a limit-structure game."

**Put on the Heat**

To pressure your opponents with aggressive betting strategies to get the most value from your hand. "You might consider *putting on the heat* when your opponent is slightly conservative or when he has a short stack against your big stack."

**Put Them on (a Hand)**

To assign a certain value to an opponent's hand. "Using my instincts and how he played the hand, I *put Stanley on* the nut low."

**Rag (or Blank)**

A board card that doesn't help appears not to have helped anyone at the table. "The flop came with A-2-3 and then a *rag*, the 9[, hit on the turn."

**Rag Off**

The river card doesn't help you. "Then it *ragged off* on the end and he was a gone goose for all his money."

**Rainbow Flop**

The flop cards are three different suits. "I liked my straight draw when the flop came *rainbow* and nobody could have a flush draw against me."

**Read the Board**

To understand the value of your hand in relation to the cards on the board. "If you *read the board* correctly, you often can tell where you're at in the hand by the action."

**Round**

The predetermined length of time that each betting increment is in force during a tournament (30 minutes, one hour, and so on). "At the end of the $25/$50 *round*, I had $3,000 in chips going into the $50/$100 *round*."

**Run Over**

To play aggressively in an attempt to control the other players. "If they're not trying to stop you from being a bully, then keep *running over them* until they do."

**Runner-Runner**

To catch cards on the turn and river that make your hand a winner. "As it turns out, you had a suited K-J, caught *runner-runner* to make a flush, and broke me!"

**Second-Hand Low**

To limp-in behind a raiser on the preflop, usually with aces, hoping that a player behind reraises, so that you can come over the top of him. "With pocket aces in middle position, I played *second-hand low* and just called the early raiser to try to trap him."

**Showdown**

When no one bets at the river and the cards are turned over to determine the winner. "If everyone checks to you at the river and you couldn't win in a *showdown*, why bet if you know that you will get called?"

**Shut Down**

To stop playing aggressively. "When the board paired the second highest card, I decided to *shut down*."

**Slowplay**

To refrain from betting a strong hand for maximum value because you are hoping to trap your opponents. "I knew the rock in the third seat was *slowplaying* aces so I didn't bet my set when he checked on the flop."

**Smooth Call**

To call a bet without raising. "If someone bets into you, you might *smooth call* with this type of hand because you have an extra out."

**Solid Player**

An accomplished player who employs the right strategy at all times. "I decided not to call Boston's raise because I knew he was a *solid player* who wouldn't get out of line."

**Stand a Raise**

To call a raise. "I recently *stood a raise* in a cash game with 9-8 on the button. The board came 7-6-2, no suits. A guy led off with a decent bet and I called him with my overcards and a straight draw."

**Stiffed In**

To play a blind hand in an unraised pot. "The only time that you might play 7-2 in hold'em is when you are *stiffed in* in the big blind."

**Surrender**

To give up on your hand. "When the fourth flush card hit at the river, I had to *surrender*."

**Survival Tactics**

To play conservatively rather than bet for maximum value in an attempt to last longer in the tournament. "I couldn't risk losing too many chips with my short stack, so I just called instead of raising, using *survival tactics* to make it to the final table."

**Take off a Card**

To call a bet on the flop. "I decided to *take off a card* and see what the turn would bring."

**Takeoff Hand**

A hand that has the potential to beat a better starting hand because it's live. "In four-way action, I figured that my middle connectors might turn into a *takeoff hand*."

**Take Them Off (a hand)**

To beat a superior starting hand. "Any of those types of hands in which you have two straight cards and a pair will *take the aces right off* a lot of times."

**Tell**

A mannerism that a player exhibits at the table that tips off an opponent to what he's holding or how he's likely to play the hand. "I'd seen Nick hesitate in betting when he had a big hand, so when he paused before pushing in his chips, it was a definite *tell*."

## Underpair

A pair that is lower than a pair showing on the board. "Why would you ever want to call with an *underpair*?"

## Wake Up With a Hand

You are dealt a hand with winning potential. "Just because a player is a maniac doesn't mean that he can't *wake up with a hand*. Over the long haul, everybody gets the same number of good hands and bad hands."

## Weak Ace

You have an ace in your hand but you do not have a high kicker to go with it. "I won't bet a *weak ace* unless I am certain that I have the only ace at the table."

## Where You're At

You understand the value of your hand in relation to the other players' hands. "Your opponent may not know for sure where you're at in the hand when you have played it in a deceptive way."

# GREAT CARDOZA POKER BOOKS
## ADD THESE TO YOUR LIBRARY - ORDER NOW!

**DANIEL NEGREANU'S POWER HOLD'EM STRATEGY** *by Daniel Negreanu.* This power-packed book on beating no-limit hold'em is one of the three most influential poker books ever written. Negreanu headlines a collection of young great players—Todd Brunson, David Williams. Erick Lindgren, Evelyn Ng and Paul Wasicka—who share their insider professional moves and winning secrets. You'll learn about short-handed and heads-up play, high-limit cash games, a powerful beginner's strategy to neutralize pro players, and how to mix up your play, bluff and win big pots. The centerpiece, however, is Negreanu's powerful and revolutionary small ball strategy. You'll learn how to play hold'em with cards you never would have played before—and with fantastic results. The preflop, flop, turn and river will never look the same again. A must-have! 520 pages, $34.95.

**POKER WIZARDS** *by Warwick Dunnett.* In the tradition of Super System, an exclusive collection of champions and superstars have been brought together to share their strategies, insights, and tactics for winning big money at poker, specifically no-limit hold'em tournaments. This is priceless advice from players who individually have each made millions of dollars in tournaments, and collectively, have won more than 20 WSOP bracelets, two WSOP main events, 100 major tournaments and $50 million in tournament winnings! Featuring Daniel Negreanu, Dan Harrington, Marcel Luske, Kathy Liebert, Mike Sexton, Mel Judah, Marc Salem, T.J Cloutier and Chris "Jesus" Ferguson. This must-read book is a goldmine for all serious players, aspiring pros, and future champions! 352 pgs, $19.95.

**HOLD'EM WISDOM FOR ALL PLAYERS** *by Daniel Negreanu.* Superstar poker player Daniel Negreanu provides 50 easy-to-read and right-to-the-point hold'em strategy nuggets that will immediately make you a better player at cash games and tournaments. His wit and wisdom makes for great reading; even better, it makes for killer winning advice. Conversational, straightforward, and educational, this book covers topics as diverse as the top 10 rookie mistakes to bullying bullies and exploiting your table image. 176 pages, $14.95.

**OMAHA HIGH-LOW: How to Win at the Lower Limits** *by Shane Smith.* Practical advice specifically targeted for the popular low-limit games you play every day in casinos and online will have you making money, and show you how to avoid losing situations and cards that can cost you a bundle—the dreaded second-nut draws, trap hands, and two-way second-best action. Smith's proven strategies are spiced with plenty of wit and wisdom. You'll learn the basics of play against the typical opponents you'll face in low-limit games—the no-fold'em players and the rocks—and get winning tactics, illustrated hands, and tournament tips guaranteed to improve your game. 144 pages, $12.95.

**MORE HOLD'EM WISDOM FOR ALL PLAYERS** *by Daniel Negreanu.* Immediately learn how to improve your hold'em game. Built on 50 concepts and strategies covered in his first book, *Hold'em Wisdom for All Players*, Daniel Negreanu offers 50 new and powerful tips to help you win money at hold'em cash and tournament games! If you love playing poker, you owe it to yourself to explore new ideas, learn more way to polish your skills, and get the most enjoyment you can from the game. See you at the felt! 176 pages; $14.95.

**NO-LIMIT TEXAS HOLD 'EM** *by Brad Daugherty & Tom McEvoy.* New Edition! Twelve power-packed courses cover the full gamut of winning no-limit hold'em tournaments! Two World Champions of Poker, Brad Daugherty and Tom McEvoy, the "Champion of Champions," give you unmatched practical advice on how to beat the low buy-in tournaments played everywhere. Includes more than 70 play-by-play examples using all the key hand categories. Learn how to make the right decision from two proven winners. 224 pages, $19.95.

# DOYLE BRUNSON'S EXCITING BOOKS
## ADD THESE TO YOUR COLLECTION - ORDER NOW!

**SUPER SYSTEM** by *Doyle Brunson*. This classic book is considered by the pros to be the best book ever written on poker! Jam-packed with advanced strategies, theories, tactics and money-making techniques, no serious poker player can afford to be without this hard-hitting information. Includes fifty pages of the most precise poker statistics ever published. Features chapters written by poker's biggest superstars, such as Dave Sklansky, Mike Caro, Chip Reese, Joey Hawthorne, Bobby Baldwin, and Doyle. Essential strategies, advanced play, and no-nonsense winning advice on making money at 7-card stud (razz, high-low split, cards speak, and declare), draw poker, lowball, and hold'em (limit and no-limit).This is a must-read for any serious poker player. 628 pages, $29.95.

**SUPER SYSTEM 2** by *Doyle Brunson*. SS2 expands upon the original with more games and professional secrets from the best in the world. New revision includes Phil Hellmuth Jr. along with superstar contributors Daniel Negreanu, winner of multiple WSOP gold bracelets and 2004 Poker Player of the Year; Lyle Berman, 3-time WSOP gold bracelet winner, founder of the World Poker Tour, and super-high stakes cash player; Bobby Baldwin, 1978 World Champion; Johnny Chan, 2-time World Champion and 10-time WSOP bracelet winner; Mike Caro, poker's greatest researcher, theorist, and instructor; Jennifer Harman, the world's top female player and one of ten best overall; Todd Brunson, winner of more than 20 tournaments; and Crandell Addington, no-limit hold'em legend. 704 pgs, $29.95.

**CARO'S GUIDE TO DOYLE BRUNSON'S SUPER SYSTEM** by *Mike Caro*. Working with World Champion Doyle Brunson, the legendary Mike Caro has created a fresh look to the "Bible" of all poker books, adding new and personal insights that help you understand the original work. Caro breaks 36 concepts into either "Analysis, Commentary, Concept, Mission, Play-By-Play, Psychology, Statistics, Story, or Strategy. Lots of illustrations and winning concepts give even more value to this great work. 86 pages, 8 1/2 x 11, $19.95.

**ACCORDING TO DOYLE** by *Doyle Brunson*. Learn what it takes to be a great poker player by climbing inside the mind of poker's most famous champion. Fascinating anecdotes and adventures from Doyle's early career playing poker in roadhouses are interspersed with lessons from the champion who has made more money at poker than anyone else in history. Learn what makes a great player tick, how he approaches the game, and receive candid, powerful advice from the legend himself. 208 pages, $14.95.

**MY 50 MOST MEMORABLE HANDS** by *Doyle Brunson*. This instant classic relives the most incredible hands by the greatest poker player of all time. Great players, legends, and poker's most momentous events march in and out of fifty years of unforgettable hands. Sit side-by-side with Doyle as he replays the excitement and life-changing moments of the most thrilling and crucial hands in the history of poker: from his early games as a rounder in the rough-and-tumble "Wild West" years—where a man was more likely to get shot as he was to get a straight flush—to the nail-biting excitement of his two world championship titles. Relive million dollar hands and the high stakes tension of sidestepping police, hijackers and murderers. A thrilling collection of stories and sage poker advice. 168 pages, $14.95.

**THE GODFATHER OF POKER** by *Doyle Brunson*. Doyle Brunson's riveting autobiography is a story of guts and glory, of good luck and bad, of triumph and unspeakable tragedy. It is a story of beating the odds, of a man who bet $1 million on a hole of golf—when he could barely stand! A master of the bluff, here is a man whose most outrageous bluff came with a gunman pointing a pistol at his forehead. He has survived whippings, gun fights, stabbings, mobsters, killers and a bout with cancer where the doctor told him his hand was played out. Apparently, fate had never played poker with Brunson; he lived. Doyle has searched for Noah's ark, tried to raise the Titanic, and won two poker championships. A must read. 352 pages, $26.95

# GREAT CARDOZA POKER BOOKS
## POWERFUL BOOKS YOU MUST HAVE

**CARO'S MOST PROFITABLE HOLD'EM ADVICE** *by Mike Caro.* When Mike Caro writes a book on winning, all poker players take notice. And they should: The "Mad Genius of Poker" has influenced just about every professional player and world champion alive. You'll journey far beyond the traditional tactical tools offered in most poker books and for the first time, have access to the entire missing arsenal of strategies left out of everything you've ever seen or experienced. Caro's first major work in two decades is packed with hundreds of powerful ideas, concepts, and strategies, many of which will be new to you—they have never been made available to the general public. This book represents Caro's lifelong research into beating the game of hold em. 408 pages, $24.95

**CARO'S BOOK OF POKER TELLS** *by Mike Caro.* One of the ten greatest books written on poker, this must-have book should be in every player's library. If you're serious about winning, you'll realize that most of the profit comes from being able to read your opponents. Caro reveals the secrets of interpreting *tells*—physical reactions that reveal information about a player's cards—such as shrugs, sighs, shaky hands, eye contact, and many more. Learn when opponents are bluffing, when they aren't and why—based solely on their mannerisms. Over 170 photos of players in action and play-by-play examples show the actual tells. These powerful ideas will give you the decisive edge. 320 pages, $24.95.

**THE POKER TOURNAMENT FORMULA** *by Arnold Snyder.* Start making money now in fast no-limit hold'em tournaments with these radical and never-before-published concepts and secrets for beating tournaments. You'll learn why cards don't matter as much as the dynamics of a tournament—your position, the size of your chip stack, who your opponents are, and above all, the structure. Poker tournaments offer one of the richest opportunities to come along in decades. Every so often, a book comes along that changes the way players attack a game and provides them with a big advantage over opponents. Gambling legend Arnold Snyder has written such a book. 368 pages, $19.95.

**POKER TOURNAMENT FORMULA 2: Advanced Strategies for Big Money Tournaments** *by Arnold Snyder.* Probably the greatest tournament poker book ever written, and the most controversial in the last decade, Snyder's revolutionary work debunks commonly (and falsely) held beliefs. Snyder reveals the power of chip utility—the real secret behind winning tournaments—and covers utility ranks, tournament structures, small- and long-ball strategies, patience factors, the impact of structures, crushing the Harringbots and other player types, tournament phases, and much more. Includes big sections on Tools, Strategies, and Tournament Phases. A must buy! 496 pages, $24.95.

**OMAHA HIGH-LOW: Play to Win with the Odds** *by Bill Boston.* Selecting the right hands to play is the most important decision to make in Omaha. This is the *only* book that shows you the chances that every one of the 5,278 Omaha high-low hands has of winning the high end of the pot, the low end of it, and how often it is expected to scoop all the chips. You get all the vital tools needed to make critical preflop decisions based on the results of more than 500 million computerized hand simulations. You'll learn the 100 most profitable starting cards, trap hands to avoid, 49 worst hands, 30 ace-less hands you can play for profit, and the three bandit cards you must know to avoid losing hands. 248 pages, $19.95.

**HOW TO BEAT SIT-AND-GO POKER TOURNAMENTS** by Neil Timothy. There is a lot of dead money up for grabs in the lower limit sit-and-gos and Neil Timothy shows you how to go and get it. The author, a professional player, shows you how to reach the last six places of lower limit sit-and-go tournaments four out of five times and then how to get in the money 25-35 percent of the time using his powerful, proven strategies. This book can turn a losing sit-and-go player into a winner, and a winner into a bigger winner. Also effective for the early and middle stages of one-table satellites.176 pages, $14.95.

# THE CHAMPIONSHIP SERIES
## POWERFUL INFORMATION YOU MUST HAVE

**CHAMPIONSHIP NO-LIMIT & POT-LIMIT HOLD'EM** by *T. J. Cloutier & Tom McEvoy.* New edition! The bible for winning pot-limit and no-limit hold'em gives you the answers to your most important questions: How do you get inside your opponents' heads and learn how to beat them at their own game? How can you tell how much to bet, raise, and reraise in no-limit hold'em? When can you bluff? How do you set up your opponents in pot-limit hold'em so that you can win a monster pot? What are the best strategies for winning no-limit and pot-limit tournaments, satellites, and supersatellites? Rock-solid and inspired advice you can bank on from two of the most recognizable figures in poker. 304 pages, $19.95.

**CHAMPIONSHIP HOLD'EM** by *T. J. Cloutier & Tom McEvoy.* New edition! Hard-hitting hold'em the way it's played *today* in both limit cash games and tournaments. Get killer advice on how to win more money in rammin'-jammin' games, kill-pot, jackpot, shorthanded, and full table cash games. You'll learn the thinking process for preflop, flop, turn, and river play with specific suggestions for what to do when good or bad things happen. Includes play-by-play analyses, advice on how to maximize profits against rocks in tight games, weaklings in loose games, experts in solid games, plus tournament strategies for small buy-in, big buy-in, rebuy, satellite and big-field major tournaments. Wow! 392 pages, $19.95.

**CHAMPIONSHIP OMAHA (Omaha High-Low, Pot-limit Omaha, Limit High Omaha)** by *Tom McEvoy & T.J. Cloutier.* New edition! Clearly-written strategies and powerful advice from Cloutier and McEvoy who have won four World Series of Poker Omaha titles. You'll learn how to beat low-limit and high-stakes games, play against loose and tight opponents, and the differing strategies for rebuy and freezeout tournaments. Learn the best starting hands, when slowplaying a big hand is dangerous, what danglers are (and why winners don't play them), why you sometimes fold the nuts on the flop and would be correct in doing so, and overall, how you can win a lot of money at Omaha! 272 pages, illustrations, $19.95.

**CHAMPIONSHIP 107 HOLD'EM TOURNAMENT HANDS** by *T. J. Cloutier & Tom McEvoy.* An absolute must for hold'em tournament players, two legends show you how to become a winning tournament player at both limit and no-limit hold'em games. Get inside the authors' heads as they think their way through the correct strategy at limit and no-limit starting hands. Cloutier & McEvoy show you how to use skill and intuition to play strategic hands for maximum profit in real tournament scenarios and how key hands were played by champions in turnaround situations at the WSOP. Gain tremendous insights into how tournament poker is played at the highest levels. 352 pages, $19.95.

**CHAMPIONSHIP HOLD'EM SATELLITE STRATEGY** by *World Champions Brad Daugherty & Tom McEvoy.* Every year satellite players win their way into the $10,000 WSOP buy-in and emerge as millionaires or champions. You can too! Learn the specific, proven strategies for winning almost any satellite from two world champions. Covers the ten ways to win a seat at the WSOP, how to win limit hold'em and no-limit hold'em satellites, one-table satellites, online satellites, and the final table of super satellites. Includes a special chapter on no-limit hold'em satellites! 320 pages, $29.95.

**HOW TO WIN THE CHAMPIONSHIP: Hold'em Strategies for the Final Table,** by *T.J. Cloutier.* If you're hungry to win a championship, this is the book that will pave the way! T.J. Cloutier, the greatest tournament poker player ever—he has won 60 major tournament titles and appeared at 39 final tables at the WSOP, both more than any other player in the history of poker—shows you how to get to the final table where the big money is made and then how to win it all. You'll learn how to build up enough chips to make it through the early and middle rounds and then how to employ T.J.'s own strategies to outmaneuver opponents at the final table and win championships. You'll learn how to adjust your play depending upon stack sizes, antes/blinds, table position, opponents styles, chip counts, and the specific strategies for six-handed, three handed, and heads-up play. 288 pages, $29.95.

**Order now at 1-800-577-WINS or go online to: www.cardozabooks.com**

# POWERFUL WINNING POKER SIMULATIONS
## A MUST FOR SERIOUS PLAYERS WITH A COMPUTER!
### IBM compatible CD ROM Win 95, 98, 2000, NT, ME, XP

These incredible full color poker simulations are the best method to improve your game. Computer opponents play like real players. All games let you set the limits and rake and have fully programmable players, plus stat tracking, and Hand Analyzer for starting hands. Mike Caro, the world's foremost poker theoretician says, "Amazing... a steal for under $500... get it, it's great." Includes free phone support. "Smart Advisor" gives expert advice for every play!

**1. TURBO TEXAS HOLD'EM FOR WINDOWS - $59.95.** Choose which players, and how many (2-10) you want to play, create loose/tight games, and control check-raising, bluffing, position, sensitivity to pot odds, and more! Also, instant replay, pop-up odds, Professional Advisor keeps track of play statistics. Free bonus: Hold'em Hand Analyzer analyzes all 169 pocket hands in detail and their win rates under any conditions you set. Caro says this "hold'em software is the most powerful ever created." Great product!

**2. TURBO SEVEN-CARD STUD FOR WINDOWS - $59.95.** Create any conditions of play; choose number of players (2-8), bet amounts, fixed or spread limit, bring-in method, tight/loose conditions, position, reaction to board, number of dead cards, and stack deck to create special conditions. Features instant replay. Terrific stat reporting includes analysis of starting cards, 3-D bar charts, and graphs. Play interactively and run high speed simulation to test strategies. Hand Analyzer analyzes starting hands in detail. Wow!

**3. TURBO OMAHA HIGH-LOW SPLIT FOR WINDOWS - $59.95.** Specify any playing conditions; betting limits, number of raises, blind structures, button position, aggressiveness/passiveness of opponents, number of players (2-10), types of hands dealt, blinds, position, board reaction, and specify flop, turn, and river cards! Choose opponents and use provided point count or create your own. Statistical reporting, instant replay, pop-up odds high speed simulation to test strategies, amazing Hand Analyzer, and much more!

**4. TURBO OMAHA HIGH FOR WINDOWS - $59.95.** Same features as above, but tailored for Omaha High only. Caro says program is "an electrifying research tool...it can clearly be worth thousands of dollars to any serious player. A must for Omaha High players.

**5. TURBO 7 STUD 8 OR BETTER - $59.95.** Brand new with all the features you expect from the Wilson Turbo products: the latest artificial intelligence, instant advice and exact odds, play versus 2-7 opponents, enhanced data charts that can be exported or printed, the ability to fold out of turn and immediately go to the next hand, ability to peek at opponents hand, optional warning mode that warns you if a play disagrees with the advisor, and automatic mode that runs up to 50 tests unattended. Tough computer players vary their styles for a great game.

---

## 6. TOURNAMENT TEXAS HOLD'EM - $39.95

Set-up for tournament practice and play, this realistic simulation pits you against celebrity look-alikes. Tons of options let you control tournament size with 10 to 300 entrants, select limits, ante, rake, blind structures, freezeouts, number of rebuys and competition level of opponents. Pop-up status report shows how you're doing vs. the competition. Save tournaments in progress to play again later. Additional feature allows quick folds on finished hands.

---

AUG 2 3 2021